Forgotten Lancashire
Folk and Fairy Tales

Compiled by
Andrew Walsh

Published by Innovative Libraries Press
195 Wakefield Road, Lepton, Huddersfield. HD8 0BL.
Andywalsh999@gmail.com
First Published 2020

ISBN (Paperback): 9781911500162
ISBN (ebook): 9781911500179

Contents

Introduction...5

Mossycoat...7

Th' Skriker...9

The Unbidden Guest...13

The Fairy's Spade...22

The King of the Fairies...24

Mother and Child...29

The Spectral Cat...32

The Captured Fairies..39

The Pillion Lady...42

The Fairy Funeral...45

The Chivalrous Devil...53

The Enchanted Fisherman....................................57

The Sands of Cocker..68

The Silver Token..74

The Headless Woman...76

The Rescue of Moonbeam....................................81

The White Dobbie..89

The Little Man's Gift...94

Satan's Supper...97

The Earthenware Goose......................................102

The Phantom of the Fell.....................................107

Allhallow's Night...117

The Christmas Eve Vigil.....................................123

The Crier of Claife...132

The Demon of the Oak...138

The Black Cock..146

The Invisible Burden...149

The Boggart in Top Attic..153

A Cure for Toothache...155

Silken Janet (or Mucketty Meg) 156

Dule upon Dun..160

Nut Nan and more..162

The Devil and the Tailor 164

Fairest of all others 168

The Clever Little Tailor 170

The Bottle of Water from the World's End Well..........172

Lousy Jack and his Eleven Brothers.................................174

The Man Who Didn't Believe in Ghosts and 'chantments
....176

The Dragon of Wantley...178

Dildrum, King of the Cats..180

A Fairy Changeling..181

A Fairy Experience..182

The Goodwife of Deloraine...184

Loynd in the Vale of Todmorden.....................................186

The Barcroft Boggart...191

Halstead Changeling..193

Alderman & Alphin..195

Main Sources...197

Introduction

Welcome to this collection of Lancashire folk and fairy tales. They've come from a range of old sources, and some might be familiar to readers as they've cropped up in other collections, or been adapted over the years. Many may be completely new to you, as we seem to be exposed to a much smaller collection of fairy tales when young these days, often dominated by telling after retelling of a small number of popular tales (particularly those that have been used to inspire films).

Rather than retelling them, these are largely as I've found them. I might have softened the dialect in a few (though not all), particularly where there was large stretches of dialect conversations, tending to just leave short asides in dialect, in the hope that these are easier to read than when they are a large proportion of a story. A few I have very slightly expanded that I found only in note form, but I've tried to be as true as possible to the stories as I found them. As such, there are a range of voices and styles, and some seem a little confused at times!

The key sources I used are listed towards the back of the book. I chose to include anything that was either clearly identified with Lancashire place names, or which had been flagged as being gathered in Lancashire by a folklorist.

I've no doubt missed many tales, especially as there were many creatures that I read mentions of, but not actual stories. For example, Jinny (or Jenny) Greenteeth lives in many Lancashire waters, ready to drag unwary people down under the surface. She's even mentioned in place names across the county, but I couldn't find a story focussing on her. The same with many boggarts (and I do love a boggart story), where I couldn't find as many as I expected, especially as you often find a boggart associated with a place name, but not a real story underneath it.

I've also missed a large source of tales out completely – John Roby's "Traditions of Lancashire". As far as I can tell, instead of telling (or retelling) Lancashire stories as he heard them, he took elements of them and redid them as high (early 19th Century) literature. Each story became *incredibly* long and flowery in style, to such an extent that any original folklore felt lost inside it. I did try and extract a core of a story from some of his "traditions", but I'm afraid I failed. Just to give a flavour of this, John Roby's version of "Dule upon Dun" is well over 5,000 words long – the version I've given in this book (from a different source) is 282 words!

Anyway, I hope you enjoy this collection of stories and maybe even adapt them to tell to other people, helping to keep a little bit of them alive.

Mossycoat

A hawker wanted to marry a widow's young daughter, but she did not want to marry him and wasn't sure what to do about it. The widow, who was part way through spinning a coat for her, told her to try and get as much out of him while she finished spinning the coat, after which she'd have no need of him anyway. She told her first to ask him for a white satin dress with sprigs of gold as big as her hand, which must fit her exactly. The girl did so, and three days later, the hawker brought it to her.

The girl asked her mother what to do next, and at her instruction, asked the hawker for a silk dress the colour of all the birds of the air, which must fit her exactly. When he brought that, a few days later, she asked for silver slippers, which again, must fit her exactly. When he did that too, her mother told him to come the next day, at ten o'clock, to get his answer. Before he arrived, the mother gave her the coat, which she had made of moss and gold thread, which would let her move anywhere else by wishing and also to change herself into any form by wishing. Then she told her to wish herself 100 miles away, where she would find a great hall in which she would find work.

She tried to get a job as a cook, but though they already had a cook, the lady of the house offered to hire her to help as the undercook. She took the job, but the other servants would not put up with it, being jealous of her beauty and her getting such a position from walking straight in off the road; instead, they made her clean dishes and hit her on the head with the stock skimmer.

After a while, a dance was organised at the hall, but the other servants jeered at the idea that she might go. The young master, who had seen how beautiful she was, asked her if she wanted to go with him, but she said she was too dirty, even when the master and mistress encouraged her as well. That night, however, she put all the other servants magically asleep, washed, put on the white satin dress, and used the mossycoat to go to the ball. The young master fell in love with her, but she said only that she came from a place where people hit her on the head with a skimmer, and when the ball was over, she used the mossycoat to go back. She woke all the servants and hinted she might have to tell the mistress about their sleeping, so they treated her better for a short while. It didn't last long though, and they heard the story of the grand lady who'd impressed the young master at the ball, they went back to abusing her.

Another ball came along, and this time, she went in the other dress. The young master tried to catch her, and perhaps touched her shoe; at any rate, it came off. He made every woman try to put on the shoe, and when he heard that Mossycoat alone had not tried it, he sent for her too. The shoe fit her perfectly. The master and mistress told off the servants for hitting her with the skimmer, and the young master and Mossycoat were married.

Th' Skriker[1]

On a fine night, about the middle of December, many years ago, a sturdy-looking young fellow left Chipping for his cottage, three or four miles away, upon the banks of the Hodder. The ground was covered with snow, which in many places had drifted into heaps, and the keen frost had made the road so slippery that the progress he made was slow. Nature looked very beautiful, and the heart of the rustic was touched by the sweet peacefulness of the scene.

Adam was not easily scared, but there was a nameless something in the deathly silence which oppressed, if it did not actually frighten, him; and although he sang aloud a verse of the last song he had heard before he left the kitchen of the Patten Arms, his voice had lost its heartiness. He earnestly wished himself safely across the little bridge over the brook; but he was yet some distance from the stream when the faint chimes of midnight fell upon the air. Almost immediately after the last stroke of twelve had broken the silence a cloud passed over the face of the moon, and the darkness deepened; the wind, which before had been gentle and almost noiseless, began to howl amid the boughs and branches of the waving trees, and the frozen snow from the hedgerows was dashed against the wayfarer's face.

He had already begun to fancy that he could hear unearthly cries and fiendish shouts of glee in the wind; but as he approached the stream his courage almost

---

[1] Shrieker

entirely failed him, and it required a great effort to keep from running back to the Patten Arms. He reassured himself that if he could only cross the bridge he would be safe, the Greenies, Boggarts, and Feorin not having power over any one who had passed over the water. He carried on, and had almost reached the bridge when he heard the noise of passing feet in the crunching snow, and became conscious of the presence of a ghastly thing he was unable to see.

Suddenly a sepulchral howl brought him to a stop, and, with his heart throbbing loudly enough to be heard, he stood gazing fixedly into the darkness. There was nothing to be seen, however, but the bridge; and he might have stood there until daylight had not another cry, louder and even more unearthly and horrible than the preceding one, called him from his trance.

No sooner had this second scream died away than, impelled by an irresistible impulse, he stepped forward in the direction whence the noise had come. At this moment the moon burst forth from behind the clouds which had for some time obscured her light, and her rays fell upon the road, with its half-hidden cart-tracks winding away into the dim distance; and in the very centre of the bridge he beheld a hideous figure with black shaggy hide, and huge eyes closely resembling orbs of fire.

Adam at once knew from the likeness the dread object bore to the figure he had heard described by those who had seen the Skriker, that the terrible thing before him was an Ambassador of Death.

Without any consciousness of what he was doing, and acting as though under the sway of a strange and irresistible mesmeric influence, he stepped towards the bridge; but no sooner did he stir than the frightful thing in front of him, with a motion that was not walking, but rather a sort of heavy gliding, moved also, slowly retreating, pausing when he paused, and always keeping its fiery eyes fixed upon his blanched face. Slowly he crossed the stream, but gradually his steps grew more and more rapid, until he broke into a run.

He ran for perhaps a mile, when suddenly he stumbled over a stone and fell. In a second, impressed by a fear that the ghastly object would seize him, he regained his feet, and, to his intense relief, the Skriker was no longer visible. With a sigh of pleasure he sat down upon a heap of broken stones, for his limbs, refused to bear him further for a few moments. After a short rest, he slowly trudged along once more.

As he got closer to home, once more the terrible shriek rang out. When he reached the old bridge spanning the Hodder, once more he saw, in the centre of the road, about midway of the stream, the same terrible object he had followed along the lane from the brook at Thornley.

Terrified once more, he felt compelled to run again. The distance home was covered fast, and the Skriker, with its face towards the terrified man, took up its position against the door of the dwelling. Adam could not resist the attraction which drew him to the ghastly thing, and as he neared it, in a fit of wild desperation, he struck at it, but his hand banged against the oak of the door, and, as the spectre splashed away, he fell forward in a faint.

Disturbed by the noise of the fall, the goodwife arose and drew him into the cottage, but for some hours he was unable to tell the story of his terrible journey. When he had told of his involuntary chase of the Skriker, a deep gloom fell over the woman's features, for she well knew what the ghastly visit portended to their little household. The dread uncertainty did not continue long, however, for on the third day from that upon which Adam had reached his home the eldest lad was brought home drowned; and after attending the child's funeral, Adam's wife sickened of a fever, and within a few weeks she too was carried to Mytton churchyard.

The Unbidden Guest

In a little lane leading from the town of Clitheroe there once lived a noted 'cunning man,' to whom all sorts of applications were made, not only by the residents, but also by people from distant places, for the fame of the wizard had spread over the whole country side.

If a theft was committed, at once the services of 'Owd Jeremy' were enlisted, and, as a result, some one entirely innocent was, if not accused, at least suspected; while maidens and young men, anxious to pry into futurity, and behold the faces of their unknown admirers, paid him trifling fees to enable them to gratify their curiosity. In short, Jeremy professed to be an able student of the Black Art, on familiar speaking terms with Satan, and duly qualified to foretell men's destinies by the aid of the stars.

The cottage in which the old man resided was of a mean order, and its outward appearance was by no means likely to impress visitors with an idea that great pecuniary advantages had followed that personal acquaintance with the Evil One of which the wizard boasted.

If, however, the outside was mean and shabby, the inside of the dwelling was of a nature better calculated to inspire inquirers with feelings of awe, hung round, as the one chamber was, with faded and moth-eaten black cloth, upon which grotesque astrological designs and the figure of a huge dragon were worked in flaming red.

The window being hidden by the dingy tapestry, the only light in the room came from a starved-looking candle, which was fixed in the foot of the skeleton of a child, attached to a string from the ceiling, and dangling just over the table, where a ponderous volume lay open before a large crystal globe and two skulls.

In an old-fashioned chair, above which hung suspended a dirty and dilapidated crocodile, the wizard sat, and gave audience to the stray visitors whose desire to peer into futurity overmastered the fear with which the lonely cottage was regarded.

A quaint-looking old man was Jeremy, with his hungry-looking eyes and long white beard; and, as with bony fingers he turned over the leaves of the large book, there was much in his appearance likely to give the superstitious and ignorant customers overwhelming ideas of his wondrous wisdom. The 'make up' was creditable to Jeremy, for though he succeeded in deceiving others with his assumption of supernatural knowledge, he himself did not believe in those powers whose aid he so frequently professed to invoke on behalf of his clients.

One day, when the ragged cloth had fallen behind a victim who was departing from the wizard's sanctum with a few vague and mysterious hints in exchange for solid coin, the old man, after laughing sarcastically, pulled aside the dingy curtains and stepped to the casement, through which the glorious sunlight was streaming. The scene upon which the wizard looked was a very beautiful one; and the old man leaned his head upon his hands and gazed intently upon the landscape.

'Tis a bonnie world,' said he,—'tis a bonnie world, and there are few views in it to compare with this one for beauty. My soul is drawn toward old Pendle, yon, with a love passing that of woman, heartless and passionless though the huge mass be. Heartless!' said he, after a pause,—'heartless! when every minute there is a fresh expression upon its beautiful front? Ay, even so, for it looms yonder calm and unconcerned when we are ushered into the world, and when we are ushered out of it, and laid to moulder away under the mountain's shadow; and it will rear its bold bluffs to heaven and smile in the sunlight or frown in the gloom after we who now love to gaze upon it are blind to the solemn loveliness of its impassable face. Poor perishable fools are we, with less power than the breeze which ruffles yon purple heather!'

With a heavy sigh Jeremy turned away from the window, and as the curtain fell behind him, and he stood again in the wretchedly-lighted room, he saw that he was not alone. The chair in which the trembling hinds generally were asked to seat themselves held a strange-looking visitor of dark and forbidding aspect.

'Jeremiah,' said this personage, 'devildom first and poetising afterwards.'

There was an unpleasant tone of banter in this speech, which did not seem in keeping with the character of one who fain would pry into futurity; and as the wizard took his usual position beneath the crocodile, he looked somewhat less oracular than was his wont when in front of a shivering and terrified inquirer.

'What wantest thou with me?' said he, with an ill-assumed appearance of unconcern.

The occupant of the chair smiled sardonically as he replied—

'A little security—that's all. For five-and-twenty years thou hast been amassing wealth by duping credulous fools, and it is time I had my percentage.'

The wizard stared in astonishment. Was the stranger a thief, or worse? he wondered, but after a time, however, he said, drily—

'Even if thou hadst proved thy right to a portion of the profits of my honest calling—and thou hast not—thou wouldst not require a packhorse to carry thy share away. Doth this hovel resemble the abode of a possessor of great wealth? Two chairs, a table, and a few old bones, its furniture; and its tenant a half-starved old man, who has had hard work to support life upon the pittance he receives in return for priceless words of wisdom! Thou art a stranger to me, and thy portion of my earnings is correctly represented by a circle.'

A loud and unmusical laugh followed the wizard's words; and before the unpleasant sound had died away the visitor remarked—

'If I am yet a stranger to thee, Jeremiah, 'tis not thy fault, for during the last quarter of a century thou hast boasted of me as thy willing servant, and extorted hard cash from thy customers upon the strength of my friendship and willingness to help thee; and now, true to thy beggarly instincts, thou wouldst deny me! But 'twill be in vain, Jeremiah—'twill be in vain! I have postponed this visit too long already to be put off with subterfuges now.'

'I repeat, I know thee not,' said the wizard, in a trembling voice. And, hurriedly rising from his chair, he flung aside the thick curtain, in order that the light of day might stream into the chamber, for a nameless fear had taken possession of him, and he did not care to remain in the darkened apartment with his suspicious visitor. To his surprise and terror, however, darkness had fallen upon the scene, and, as he gazed in alarm at the little diamond-framed window, through which so short a time before he had looked upon a fair prospect of meadow and mountain, a vivid flash of lightning darted across the heavens, and a clap of thunder burst over the cottage.

"Twill spoil good men's harvests, Jeremiah,' the stranger calmly said; 'but it need not interrupt our interesting conversation.'

Angry at the bantering manner in which the visitor spoke, the wizard flung open the door, and cried—

'Depart from my dwelling, ere I cast thee forth into the mire!'

'Surely thou wouldst not have the heart to fulfil thy threat,' said the stranger, 'although 'tis true I have but one shoe to be soiled by the mud.' And as he spoke he quietly crossed his legs, and Jeremiah perceived a hideous cloven foot.

With a groan, the wizard sank into his chair, and, deaf to the roaring of the thunder, and to the beating of the rain through the doorway, he sat helplessly gazing at his guest, whose metallic laughter rang through the room.

'Hast thou at length recognised me, Jeremiah?' asked the Evil One, after an interval, during which he had somewhat prominently displayed the hoof, and gloated over the agony its exhibition had caused his victim.

The old man was almost too terrified to answer, but at last he whispered—

'I have.'

'And thou no longer wilt refuse me the security?' hissed the tormentor, as he placed a parchment upon the table.

'What security dost thou demand?' feebly inquired the quaking wizard.

'Personal only,' said Satan. 'Put thy name to this,' and he pointed to the bond.

Jeremy pushed his chair as far from the suspicious-looking document as he could ere he replied—

'Thou shalt not have name of mine.'

He had expected that an outburst of fiendish wrath would follow this speech, but to his surprise the guest simply remarked—

'Very well, Jeremiah. By to-morrow night, however, thou shalt be exposed as the base and ignorant pretender thou art. Thou hast trespassed upon the rightful trade of my faithful servants long enough, and 'tis time I stopped thy prosperous career. Ere sunset thou shalt have a rival, who will take the bread from thy ungrateful mouth.'

After this polite speech the visitor picked up the parchment, and began to fold it in a methodical manner.

Such utterly unexpected gentlemanly behaviour somewhat reassured Jeremiah, and in a fainter voice he humbly asked what his visitor had to give in exchange for a wizard's autograph.

'Twenty-two years of such success as thou hast not even dared to dream of! No opposition—no exposure to thy miserable dupes,' readily answered Satan.

Jeremiah considered deeply. The offer undoubtedly was a tempting one, for after all, his profession had not been very lucrative, and to lose his customers, therefore, meant starvation. He was certain that if another wizard opened an establishment the people would flock to him, even through mere curiosity; but he knew what signing the bond included, and he was afraid to take the step.

After a long delay, during which Satan carefully removed a sharp stone from his hoof, Jeremiah therefore firmly said—

'Master, I'll not sign!'

Without more ado the visitor departed, and almost before he was out of sight the storm abated, and old Pendle again became visible.

A few days passed, and no one came to the dwelling of the wizard; and as such an absence of customers was very unusual, Jeremy began to fear that the supernatural stranger had not forgotten his threat. On the evening of the fifth day he crept into the little town to purchase some articles of food. Previously, whenever he had had occasion to make a similar journey, as he passed along the street the children ran away in terror, and the older people addressed him with remarkable humility; but this time, as he stepped rapidly past the houses, the youngsters went on with their games as though only an ordinary mortal went by, and a burly fellow who was leaning against a door jamb took his pipe from his mouth to cry familiarly—

'Well, Jerry, owd lad, heaw are ta'?'

These marks of waning power and fading popularity were sufficiently unmistakable; but as he was making his few purchases he was informed that a stranger, who seemed to be possessed of miraculous powers, had arrived in the town, and that many people who had been to him were going about testifying to his wonderful skill. With a heavy heart the wizard returned to his cottage. Next night a shower of stones dashed his window to pieces, and, as he peered into the moonlight lane, he saw a number of rough fellows, who evidently were waiting and watching in hopes that he would emerge from his dwelling. These were the only visitors he had during an entire week; and at length, quite prepared to capitulate, he said to himself—

'I wish I had another chance.'

No sooner had he uttered the words, than there was a sudden burst of thunder, wind roared round the house, again the clients' chair was occupied, and the parchment lay upon the table just as though it had not been disturbed.

'Art thou ready to sign?' asked Satan.

'Ay!' answered the old man.

The Evil One immediately seized the wizard's hand, upon which Jeremy gave a piercing yell, as well he might do, for the Satanic grip had forced the blood from the tips of his fingers.

'Sign!' said the Devil.

'I can't write,' said the wizard.

The Evil One forthwith took hold of one of the victim's fingers, and using it as a pen, wrote in a peculiarly neat hand 'Jeremiah Parsons, his × mark,' finishing with a fiendish flourish.

After doing this he again vacated the chair and the room as mysteriously as on the previous occasion.

The autograph-loving visitor had barely departed with the parchment ere a knock at the door was heard, and in stepped a man who wished to have the veil lifted, and who brought the pleasing news that, influenced by the reports of the opposition wizard, he had been to his house in Clitheroe, but had found it empty, the tenant having fled no one knew whither.

From that time things looked up with Jeremy, and money poured into the skulls, for people crowded from far and near to test his skill. For two-and-twenty years he flourished and was famous, but the end came. One morning, after a wild night when the winds howled round Pendle, and it seemed as though all the powers of darkness were let loose, some labourers who were going to their work were surprised to find only the ruins of the wizard's cottage.

The place had been consumed by fire; and although search was made for the magician's remains, only a few charred bones were found, and these, some averred, were not those of old Jeremy, but were relics of the dusty old skeleton and the dirty crocodile under the shadow of which the wizard used to sit.

The Fairy's Spade

"The fairies have been getting very shy since thee and me were young, Matty, lass!" said an old grey-headed man, who, smoking a long pipe, calmly sat in a shady corner of the kitchen of a Fylde country farm-house.

"Nobody seems to see them nowadays as they used to. I once had sight of one, as plain as I can see you sitting there, darning your old stocking. I was ploughing very soon after dawn, and there wasn't a sound to be heard, nothing but the noise of the ground opening up, and the chirping of a few birds waking and tuning up, and a few crows close at my heels picking up the worms.

All of a sudden, I heard somebody cry, in a voice like old Luke in the organ loft on a Sunday, "I've broken my spade!"

I lost no time turning around to see who was awake at that hour, and in our field too, and I clapped my eyes on as pretty a little lass as has ever been seen in this countryside. Old England child's bonny, you warrant me, but they're as ugly as sin compared to the face I saw that morning. They stood with their broken spade in her hand, and in the other a hammer and two or three nails, and they smiled at me, and offered me the tools, as much as to say "Now, Isaak, be good for once in your life and fettle[2] this spade for me, will you?"

---

[2] I took most of the dialect out of this story, but had to leave in the word fettle – a good word still used across Lancashire and

For a while I stood there gaping like a fool, and wondering where they could have come from, but she cried out once more, "I've broken my spade!"

So I marched up to her, took the hammer and nails, and fixed it up. It didn't take me long doing it for her, for it was just a little 'un, but when I'd done she smiled at me, and so bonny, something like you were, Margit, when old Pighead was courting you, and she gave me a handful of brass, and before I had time to say anything, she'd vanished.

That was the only fairy as ever I've seen, and maybe the only one as I'm likely to look at, for my eyesight is getting a bit dodgy recently.'

Yorkshire, meaning "to fix" and is used for everything from fixing broken tools, to cleaning up, to finishing a job...

The King of the Fairies

Many years ago there lived in a farm-house at a point of the high-road from Manchester to Stockport, where Levenshulme Church now stands, a worthy named Burton, 'Owd Dannel Burton.'

The farm held by Daniel was a model one in its way, the old man raising finer crops than any other farmer in the district. It was rumoured that Daniel was very comfortably provided for, and that a few bad years would not harm him; and so wonderfully did everything he took in hand prosper, that his 'luck' became proverbial. Such uniform prosperity could not long continue without the tongue of envy and detraction being set wagging, and the neighbours who permitted thistles to overrun their pastures whilst they gadded about to rush-bearings and wakes, finding a reproach to their idleness not only in the old man's success, but also in the careful, industrious habits of his daily life, were not slow to insinuate that there was something more than farming at the bottom of it. 'Dannel' had sold himself to Satan, said some whose pigs had faded away, and whose harvests had not been worth the gathering; and others pretended to know even the terms of the contract, and how many years the old man yet had to play on.

A few of these detractors were young men whose imaginations were not kept in sufficient control, but they grew wonderfully reserved respecting the Satanic bargain after the hearty Daniel had had an interview with them, and proved to them that he had not forgotten the use of a good tough black-thorn.

'It's nobbut luck,' philosophically remarked others, 'mebbe it'll be my turn to-morn;' but the remainder vowed that neither luck or Evil One had anything to do with it, for the success was due to the labours of Puck, King of the Fairies.

They were right. It was Puck, although no one ever knew how the old man had been able to enlist the services of so valuable an auxiliary, Daniel being strangely reticent upon the point, although generally by no means loth to speak of the fairies and their doings. Reserve with reference to these things, however, would not have availed much, for the farm labourers, the ruddy-cheeked milkmaids, and the other women-folk about the farm-house, were fond of boasting of the exploits of Puck— how during the night everything was 'cleaned up,' and all was in apple-pie order when they came into the kitchen at daybreak, the milk churned, the cows foddered, the necessary utensils filled with water from the well, the horses ready harnessed for their day's work at the plough, and even a week's threshing done and the barn left as tidy as though it had just been emptied and swept. Evidently the servant lasses had no fear of, or objection to, a hard-working supernatural visitor of this kind, but just the reverse, and many of their listeners found themselves wishing that their house, too, had its Boggart.

For so long a period did this state of things continue, each morning revealing an astounding amount of work performed by the willing and inexpensive workman, that at length the assistance was taken for granted, and as a matter of course, offering no food for surprise, although it did not cease to be a cause of envy to the neighbours.

On one occasion, however, as old Daniel was despatching a hearty and substantial breakfast, a heated labourer brought word that all the corn had been housed during the past night. The strange story was true enough, for when the old man reached the field, where on the previous evening the golden sheaves of wheat had stood, he found the expanse quite bare, and as clean as though reapers, leaders, gleaners, and geese had been carefully over it.

The harvest was in the barn, but not content with this, Daniel, illustrating the old proverb that 'much would have more,' suddenly exclaimed, 'I wonder whose horses Puck used in this work. If yon of mine, I daresay he sweated them rarely;' and away he strode towards the stable. He had not reached the fold, however, when he met Puck coming towards him, and in a fever of greedy anxiety he cried, 'Puck, I doubt thou'st spoiled yon horses!' No sooner were the words out of his mouth, however, than he saw that for once in his life he had made a mistake, for the fairy went pale with anger as he shouted in a shrill treble:—

Sheaf to field, and horse to stall,
I, the Fairy King, recall!
Never more shall drudge of mine
Stir a horse or sheaf of thine.

After which vow he at once vanished.

The old man walked home in a sorrowful mood, and actually forgot to go to the stable; but next morning early he was disturbed by a knocking at his chamber door. 'Mesthur, ger up,' cried the messenger, who on the previous day had brought the news of the housing of the corn, 'Mesthur, ger up, th' corn's back i'th' fielt.' With a groan of anguish Daniel arose, and hastily made his way to the barn. All the pile was gone, and the floor littered with straw, exactly as it was before the fairy labour had so transformed the place.

It did not take the farmer long to get over the ground between his barn and the corn-field, and arrived there he

26

found the expanse once more covered with yellow sheaves, on which the beams of the rising sun were beginning to fall. Here and there a sheaf had fallen upon the ground, and everywhere straw and ears of corn were scattered about as though the reapers had not long before left the place. The old man turned away in despair.

From that time forward there was no more work done about the farm, or the shippons, and stables; but in the house, however, the maids continued to find their tasks performed as usual.

Great were the rejoicings in the locality when the story of the sheaves became known, and it got noised about that 'Dannel's' fairy had 'fown eawt' with him. The old man became very dejected, for although he did not clearly perceive that the rupture was entirely due to his own selfish greed, he could not go about the farm without observing how much he had lost.

One summer evening in a thoughtful mood he was walking homewards, and wishing that the meadows were mown. Plunged in such reflections, he met a neighbour, who at once asked the cause of his trouble. Daniel turned to point to the meadows, and as he did so he saw the fairy, in an attitude of rapt attention, stooping behind the hedgerow as though anxious to overhear the conversation. 'Yo' miss your neet-mon?' said the neighbour. The old man thought that the time was come to make his peace with offended royalty, and with a cunning glance in the direction of the hiding-place, he answered, 'I do, Abrum, and may God bless Puck, th' King o'th' Fayrees.'

There was a startled cry from behind the hedgerow, and both men turned in that direction, but there was nothing to be observed. The fairy had vanished, never again to be seen in Daniel Burton's fields. That night the work was left undone even inside the farm-house, and thenceforward when the kitchen needed cleaning, water was wanted from the well, or when milk had to be churned, the maids had to get up early and do the work, for Puck, King of the Fairies, would not touch either mop or pail.

Mother and Child

The tenants of Plumpton Hall had retired to rest somewhat earlier than was their wont, for it was the last night of November.

The old low rooms were in darkness, and all was silent as the grave; for though the residents, unfortunately for themselves, were not asleep, they held their breath, and awaited in fear the first stroke of the hour from the old clock in the kitchen. Suddenly the sound of hurried footsteps broke the silence; but with sighs of relief the terrified listeners found that the noise was made by a belated wayfarer, almost out of his wits with fright, but who was unable to avoid passing the hall, and who, therefore, ran by the haunted building as quickly as his legs could carry him. The sensation of escape, however, was of but short duration, for the hammer commenced to strike; and no sooner had the last stroke of eleven startled the echoes than loud thuds, as of a heavy object bumping upon the stairs, were heard.

The quaking occupants of the chambers hid their heads beneath the bedclothes, for they knew that an old-fashioned oak chair was on its way down the noble staircase, and was sliding from step to step as though dragged along by an invisible being who had only one hand at liberty.

If anyone had dared to follow that chair across the wide passage and into the wainscoted parlour, he would have been startled by the sight of a fire blazing in the grate, whence, ere the servants retired, even the very embers had been removed, and in the chair, the marvellous movement of which had so frightened all the inmates of the hall, he would have seen a beautiful woman seated, with an infant at her breast.

Year after year, on wild nights, when the snow was driven against the diamond panes, and the cry of the spirit of the storm came up from the sea, the weird firelight shone from the haunted room, and through the house sounded a mysterious crooning as the unearthly visitor softly sang a lullaby to her infant.

Lads grew up into grey-headed men in the old house; and from youth to manhood, on the last night of each November, they had heard the notes, but none of them ever had caught, even when custom had somewhat deadened the terror which surrounded the events of the much-dreaded anniversary, the words of the song the ghostly woman sang.

The maids, too, had always found the grate as it was left before the visit—not a cinder or speck of dust remaining to tell of the strange fire, and no one had ever heard the chair ascend the stairs. Chair and fire and child and mother, however, were seen by many a weary wayfarer, drawn to the house by the hospitable look of the window, through which the genial glow of the burning logs shone forth into the night, but who, by tapping at the pane and crying for shelter, could not attract the attention of the pale nurse, clad in a quaint old costume with lace ruff and ruffles, and singing a mournful and melodious lullaby to the child resting upon her beautiful bosom.

Tradition tells of one of these wanderers, a footsore and miserable seafaring man on the tramp, who, attracted by the welcome glare, crept to the panes, and seeing the cosy-looking fire, and the Madonna-faced mother tenderly nursing her infant, rapped at the glass and begged for a morsel of food and permission to sleep in

the hayloft—and, finding his pleadings unanswered,
loudly cursed the woman who could sit and enjoy
warmth and comfort and turn a deaf ear to the prayers of
the homeless and hungry; upon which the seated figure
turned the weird light of its wild eyes upon him and
almost changed him to stone—a labourer, going to his
daily toil in the early morn, finding the poor wretch
gazing fixedly through the window, against which his
terror-stricken face was closely pressed, his hair turned
white by fear, and his fingers convulsively clutching the
casement.

The Spectral Cat

Long ago—so long, in fact, that the date has been lost in obscurity—the piously-inclined inhabitants of the then thickly wooded and wild country stretching from the sea-coast to Rivington Pike and Hoghton determined to erect a church at Whittle-le-Woods, and a site having been selected, the first stone was laid with all the ceremony due to so important and solemn a proceeding.

Assisted by the labours as well as by the contributions of the faithful, the good priest was in high spirits; and as the close of the first day had seen the foundations set out and goodly piles of materials brought upon the ground ready for the future, he fell asleep congratulating himself upon having lived long enough to see the wish of his heart gratified.

What was his surprise, however, when, after arising at the break of day, and immediately rushing to his window to gaze upon the work, he could not perceive either foundation or pile of stone, the field in which he expected to observe the promising outline being as green and showing as few marks of disturbance as the neighbouring ones.

'Surely I must have been dreaming,' said the good man, as he stood with rueful eyes at the little casement, 'for there are not any signs either of the gifts or the labours of the pious sons of the church.'

In this puzzled frame of mind, and with a heavy sigh, he once more courted sleep. He had not slumbered long, however, when loud knocks at the door of his dwelling and lusty cries for Father Ambrose disturbed him. Hastily attiring himself, he descended, to find a concourse of people assembled in front of the house; and no sooner had he opened the door than a mason cried out—

'Father Ambrose, where are the foundations we laid yesterday, and where is the stone from the quarry?'

'Then I did not simply dream that I had blessed the site?' said the old man, inquiringly.

Upon which there was a shout of laughter, and a sturdy young fellow asked—

'And I did not dream that I carted six loads from the quarry?'

'Th' Owd Lad's hed a hand int',' said a labourer, 'for t' fielt's as if fuut hed never stept int'.'

The priest and his people at once set off to inspect the site, and sure enough it was in the state described by the mason; cowslips and buttercups decking the expanse of green, which took different shades as the zephyr swept over it.

'Well, I'm fair capped,' said a grey-headed old farmer. 'I've hed things stown afoor today, bud they'n generally bin things wi' feathers on an' good to heyt an' not th' feaundations uv a church. Th' warlt's gerrin' ter'ble wickit. We's hev' to bi lukkin' eawt for another Noah's flood, I warrant.'

A peal of laughter followed this sally, but Father Ambrose, who was in no mood for mirth, sternly remarked—'There is something here which savoureth of the doings of Beelzebub;' and then he sadly turned away, leaving the small crowd of gossips speculating upon the events of the night. Before the father reached his dwelling, however, he heard his name called by a rustic who was running along the road.

'Father Ambrose,' cried the panting messenger, 'here's the strangest thing happened at Leyland. The foundations of a church and all sorts of building materials have been laid in a field during the night, and Adam the miller is vowing vengeance against you for having trespassed on his land.'

The priest at once returned to the little crowd of people, who still were gaping at the field from which all signs of labour had been so wonderfully removed, and bade the messenger repeat the strange story, which he did at somewhat greater length, becoming loquacious in the presence of his equals, for he enjoyed their looks of astonishment. When the astounding narrative had been told, the crowd at once started for Leyland, their pastor promising to follow after he had fortified himself with breakfast.

When the good man reached the village he had no need to inquire which was Adam the miller's field, for he saw the crowd gathered in a rich-looking meadow. As he opened the gate Adam met him, and without ceremony at once accused him of having taken possession of his field. 'Peace, Adam,' said the priest. 'The field hath been taken not by me, but by a higher power, either good or evil—I fear the latter,' and he made his way to the people. True enough, the foundations were laid as at Whittle, and even the mortar was ready for the masons. 'I am loth to think that this is a sorry jest of the Evil One,' said Father Ambrose; 'ye must help me to outwit him, and to give him his labour for his pains. Let each one carry what he can, and, doubtless, Adam will be glad to cart the remainder,'—a proposition the burly miller agreed to at once. Accordingly each of the people walked off with a piece of wood, and Adam started for his team. Before long the field was cleared, and ere sunset the foundations were again laid in the original place, and a goodly piece of wall had been built.

Grown wise by experience, the priest selected two men to watch the place during the night. Naturally enough, these worthies, who by no means liked the task, but were afraid to decline it, determined to make themselves as comfortable as they could under the circumstances.

They therefore carried to the place a quantity of food and drink, and a number of empty sacks, with which they constructed an impromptu couch near the blazing wood fire. Notwithstanding the seductive influence of the liquor, they were not troubled with much company, for the few people who resided in the vicinity did not care to remain out of doors late after what Father Ambrose had said as to the proceeding having been a joke of Satan's. The priest, however, came to see the men, and after giving them his blessing, and a few words of advice, he left them to whatever the night might bring forth. No sooner had he gone than the watchers put up some boards to shield them from the wind, and, drawing near to the cheerful fire, they began to partake of a homely but plentiful supper. Considering how requisite it was that they should be in possession of all their wits, perhaps it would have been better had not a large bottle been in such frequent requisition, for, soon after the meal was ended, what with the effects of the by-no-means weak potion, the warmth and odour sent forth by the crackling logs, and the musical moaning of the wind in the branches overhead, they began to feel drowsy, to mutter complaints against the hardship of their lot, and to look longingly upon the heap of sacks.

'If owt comes,' said the oldest of the two, 'one con see it as well as two, an' con wakken t' tother—theerfore I'm in for a nod.' And he at once flung himself upon the rude bed.

'Well,' said the younger one, who was perched upon a log close to the fire, 'hev thi own way, an' tha'll live lunger; but I'se wakken tha soon, an' hev a doze mysen. That's fair, isn't it?'

To this question there was no response, for the old man was already asleep. The younger one immediately reached the huge bottle, and after drinking a hearty draught from it placed it within reach, saying, as he did so—

'I'm nooan freetunt o' thee, as heaw it is! Thaart not Belsybub, are ta?'

Before long he bowed his head upon his hands, and gazing into the fire gave way to a pleasant train of reflections, in which the miller's daughter played a by-no-means unimportant part. In a little while he, too, began to doze and nod, and the ideas and thronging fancies soon gave way to equally delightful dreams.

Day was breaking when the pair awoke; the fire was out, and the noisy birds were chirping their welcome to the sun. For a while the watchers stared at each other with well-acted surprise.

'I'm freetunt tha's o'erslept thysel',' said the young fellow; 'and rayly I do think as I've bin noddin' a bit mysen.' And then, as he turned round, 'Why, it's gone ageean! Jacob, owd lad! th' foundation, an' th' wō's, an' o th' lots o' stooans are off t' Leyland ageean!'

The field was again clear, grass and meadow flowers covering its expanse, and after a long conference the pair determined that the best course for them to pursue would be that of immediately confessing to Father

Ambrose that they had been asleep. Accordingly they wended their way to his house, and having succeeded in arousing him, and getting him to the door, the young man informed him that once more the foundations were missing.

'What took them?' asked the priest. To which awkward query the old man replied, that they did not see anything.

'Then ye slept, did ye?' asked the Father.

'Well,' said the young man, 'we did nod a minnit or two; but we wir toired wi' watchin' so closely; an', yo' see, that as con carry th' foundations ov a church away connot hev mich trouble i' sendin' unlarnt chaps loike Jacob an' me to sleep agen eaur will.'

This ended the colloquy, for Father Ambrose laughed heartily at the ready answer. Shortly afterwards, as on the preceding day, the messenger from Leyland arrived with tidings that the walls had again appeared in Adam's field. Again they were carted back, and placed in their original position, and once more was a watch set, the priest taking the precaution of remaining with the men until near upon midnight. Almost directly after he had left the field one of the watchers suddenly started from his seat, and cried—

'See yo', yonder, there's summat wick!'

Both men gazed intently, and saw a huge cat, with great unearthly-looking eyes, and a tail with a barbed end. Without any seeming difficulty this terrible animal took up a large stone, and hopped off with it, returning almost immediately for another. This strange performance went on for some time, the two observers being nearly petrified by terror; but at length the younger one said—

'I'm like to put a stop to yon wark, or hee'll say win bin asleep ageean,' and seizing a large piece of wood he crept down the field, the old man following closely behind. When he reached the cat, which took no notice of his approach, he lifted his cudgel, and struck the animal a heavy blow on its head. Before he had time to repeat it, however, the cat, with a piercing scream, sprang upon him, flung him to the ground, and fixed its teeth in his throat. The old man at once fled for the priest. When he returned with him, cat, foundations, and materials were gone; but the dead body of the poor watcher was there, with glazed eyes, gazing at the pitiless stars.

After this terrible example of the power of the fiendish labourer it was not considered advisable to attempt a third removal, and the building was proceeded with upon the site at Leyland chosen by the spectre.

The present parish church covers the place long occupied by the original building; and although all the actors in this story passed away centuries ago, a correct likeness of the cat has been preserved, and may be seen by the sceptical.

The Captured Fairies

There once lived in the little village of Hoghton two idle, good-for-nothing fellows, who, somehow or other, managed to exist without spending the day, from morn to dewy eve, at the loom. When their more respectable neighbours were hard at work they generally were to be seen either hanging about the doorway of the little ale-house or playing at dominoes inside the old-fashioned hostelry; and many a time in broad daylight their lusty voices might be heard as they trolled forth the hearty poaching ditty,

'It's my delight, on a shiny night.'

It was understood that they had reason to sympathise with the sentiments expressed in the old ballad. Each was followed by a ragged, suspicious-looking lurcher; and as the four lounged about the place steady-going people shook their heads, and prophesied all sorts of unpleasant terminations to so unsatisfactory a career. So far as the dogs were concerned the dismal forebodings were verified, for from poaching in the society of their masters the clever lurchers took to doing a little on their own account, and both were shot in the pursuit of game by keepers, who were only too glad of an opportunity of ridding the neighbourhood of such misdirected intelligence. Soon after this unfortunate event, the two men, who themselves had a narrow escape, had their nets taken; and, as they were too poor to purchase others, and going about to borrow such articles was equivalent to accusing their friends of poaching habits, they were reduced to the necessity of using sacks whenever they visited the squire's fields.

One night, after climbing the fence and making their way to a well-stocked warren, they put in a solitary ferret and rapidly fixed the sacks over the burrows. They did not wait long in anxious expectation of an exodus before there was a frantic rush, and after hastily grasping the sacks tightly round the necks, and tempting their missionary from the hole, they crept through the hedgerow, and at a sharp pace started for home. For some time they remained unaware of the nature of their load, and they were congratulating themselves upon the success which had crowned their industry, when suddenly there came a cry from one of the prisoners, 'Dick, wheer art ta?' The poachers stood petrified with alarm; and almost immediately a voice from the other bag piped out—

'In a sack,
On a back,
Riding up Hoghton Brow.'

The terrified men at once let their loads fall, and fled at the top of their speed, leaving behind them the bags full of fairies, who had been driven from their homes by the intruding ferret. Next morning, however, the two poachers ventured to the spot where they had heard the supernatural voices. The sacks neatly folded were lying at the side of the road, and the men took them up very tenderly, as though in expectation of another mysterious utterance, and crept off with them.

Need it be said that those bags were not afterwards used for any purpose more exciting than the carriage of potatoes from the previously neglected bit of garden, the adventure having quite cured the men of any desire to 'pick up' rabbits.

Like most sudden conversions, however, that of the two poachers into hard-working weavers was regarded with suspicion by the inhabitants of the old-world village, and in self-defence the whilom wastrels were forced to tell the story of the imprisonment of the fairies. The wonderful narrative soon got noised abroad; and as the changed characters, on many a summer evening afterwards, sat hard at work in their loom-house, and, perhaps almost instinctively, hummed the old ditty,

'It's my delight, on a shiny night,'

the shock head of a lad would be protruded through the honeysuckle which almost covered the casement, as the grinning youngster, who had been patiently waiting for the weaver to commence his song and give an opportunity for the oft-repeated repartee, cried, 'Nay, it isn't thi delight; "Dick, wheer art ta?"'

The Pillion Lady

It was on a beautiful night in the middle of summer that
Humphrey Dobson, after having transacted a day's
business at Garstang market, and passed some mirthful
hours with a number of jovial young fellows in the best
parlour of the Frances Arms, with its oak furniture and
peacock feathers, mounted his steady-going mare, and set
off for home.

He had got some distance from the little town, and was
rapidly nearing a point where the road crossed a stream
said to be haunted by the spirit of a female who had been
murdered many years back; and although the moon was
shining brightly, and the lonely rider could see far before
him, there was one dark spot overshadowed by trees a
little in advance which Humphrey feared to reach. He felt
a thrill of terror as he suddenly remembered the many
strange stories told of the headless woman whose sole
occupation and delight seemed to be that of terrifying
travellers; but, with a brave endeavour to laugh off his
fears, he urged his horse forward, and attempted to troll
forth the burden of an old song:—

'He rode and he rode till he came to the dooar,
And Nell came t' oppen it, as she'd done afooar:
"Come, get off thy horse," she to him did say,
"An' put it i'th' stable, an' give it some hay."'

It would not do, however; and suddenly he put spurs to
the mare and galloped towards the little bridge. No
sooner did the horse's hoofs ring upon the stones than
Humphrey heard a weird and unearthly laugh from
beneath the arch, and, as the animal snorted and bounded
forward, the young fellow felt an icy arm glide round his
waist and a light pressure against his back. Drops of

perspiration fell from his brow, and his heart throbbed wildly, but he did not dare to look behind lest his worst fears should be verified, and he should behold 'th' boggart o'th' bruk.'

As though conscious of its ghastly burden, the old mare ran as she never had run before; the hedgerows and trees seemed to fly past, while sparks streamed from the flints in the road, and in an incredibly short space of time the farm-house was reached. Instinctively, Humphrey tried to guide the mare into the yard, but his efforts were powerless, for the terrified animal had got the bit in her teeth, and away she sped past the gateway.

As the rider was thus borne away, another sepulchral laugh broke the silence, but this time it sounded so close to the horseman's ear that he involuntarily looked round.

He found that the figure, one of whose arms was twined round his waist, was not the headless being of whom he had heard so many fearful narratives, but another and a still more terrible one, for, grinning in a dainty little hood, and almost touching his face, there was a ghastly skull, with eyeless sockets, and teeth gleaming white in the clear moonlight.

Petrified by fear, he could not turn his head away, and, as the mare bore him rapidly along, ever and anon a horrid derisive laugh sounded in his ears as for a moment the teeth parted and then closed with a sudden snap. Terrified as he was, however, he noticed that the arm which encircled his body gradually tightened around him, and putting down his hand to grasp it he found it was that of a fleshless skeleton.

How long he rode thus embraced by a spectre he knew not, but it seemed an age.

Suddenly, however, as at a turn in the road the horse stumbled and fell, Humphrey, utterly unprepared for any such occurrence, was thrown over the animal's head and stunned by the fall.

When he recovered full consciousness, it was daybreak. The sun was rising, the birds were singing in the branching foliage overhead, and the old mare was quietly grazing at a distance. With great difficulty, for he was faint through loss of blood, and lame, he got home and told his story. There were several stout men about the farm who professed to disbelieve it, and pretended to laugh at the idea of a skeleton horsewoman, who, without saying with your leave or by your leave, had ridden pillion with the young master, but it was somewhat remarkable that none of them afterwards could be induced to cross the bridge over the haunted stream after 'th' edge o' dark.'

The Fairy Funeral

There are few spots in Lancashire more likely to have been peopled by fairies than that portion of the highway which runs along the end of Penwortham wood.

At all times the locality is very beautiful, but it is especially so in summer, when the thin line of trees on the one side of the road and the rustling wood upon the other cast a welcome shade upon the traveller, who can rest against the old railings, and look down upon a rich expanse of meadow-land and corn-fields, bounded in the distance by dim, solemn-looking hills, and over the white farm-houses, snugly set in the midst of luxurious vegetation. From this vantage-ground a flight of steps leads down to the well of St. Mary, the water of which, once renowned for its miraculous efficacy, is as clear as crystal and of never-ceasing flow.

To this sacred neighbourhood thousands of pilgrims have wended their way; and although the legend of the holy well has been lost, it is easy to understand with what superstitious reverence the place would be approached by those whose faith was of a devout and unquestioning kind, and what feelings would influence those whose hearts were heavy with the weight of a great sorrow as they descended the steps worn by the feet of their countless predecessors.

From the little spring a pathway winds across meadows and through corn-fields to the sheltered village, and a little further along the highway a beautiful avenue winds from the old lodge gates to the ancient church and priory. Wide as is this road it is more than shaded by the tall trees which tower on each side, their topmost branches almost interlaced, the sunbeams passing through the green network, and throwing fantastic gleams of light upon the pathway, along which so many have been carried to the quiet God's Acre.

At the end of this long and beautiful walk stands the old priory, no longer occupied by the Benedictines from Evesham, the silvery sound of whose voices at eventide used to swell across the rippling Ribble; and, a little to the right of the pile, the Church of St. Mary, with its background of the Castle Hill.

By the foot of this Ancient British and Roman outlook there is a little farm-house, with meadow land stretching away to the broad river; and one night, fifty or sixty years ago, two men, one of whom was a local 'cow-doctor,' whose duties had compelled him to remain until a late hour, set out from this dwelling to walk home to the straggling village of Longton. It was near upon midnight when they stepped forth, but it was as light as mid-day, the moon shining in all her beauty, and casting her glamour upon the peaceful scene. So quiet was it that it seemed as though even the Zephyrs were asleep. There was not a breath of wind, and not a leaf rustled or a blade of grass stirred, and had it not been for the sounds of the footsteps of the two men, who were rapidly ascending the rough cart-track winding up the side of the hill, all would have been as still as death. The sweet silence was a fitting one, for in the graveyard by the side of the lane through which the travellers were passing, and over the low moss-covered wall of which might be seen the old-fashioned tombstones, erect like so many sentinels marking the confines of the battle-field of life, hundreds were sleeping the sleep with which only the music of the leaves, the sough of the wind, and the sigh of the sea seem in harmony.

As the two men opened the gate at the corner of the churchyard, the old clock sounded the first stroke of midnight.

'That's twelve of them,' said the oldest of the two.

'Aye, Adam,' said the other, a taller and much younger man. 'Another day's passing away, and it can't do it without telling' everybody; yet there's very few of us to take notice of it, for we cannot do to be told that time is growing short. I should think you don't care much to hear the clock strike, Adam, to judge by the colour of your hair, for you're getting very wintry looking.'

The old man chuckled at this sally, and then said, slowly and drily:—

'Speak of yourself, Robin – speak for yourself, yet why should you speak at all? Child as you are, and you are nothing but a child, clever as you fancy yourself. You're old enough to know it's not just the grey-haired ones that die first. The chicks fall from their perch more often than the old birds. There's many an old tree with nothing but a few green buds on it, to show it was young once, that is hard work to dig up as the roots are deep in the ground, and there's many young saplings that are as easy to pull up as salad. It takes lightning to kill the old oak, but a frost in March soon puts the spring flowers out of sorts. If I'm growing old, let's hope I'm ripening as well. You wouldn't be the first lad who'd hardly finished his baby cries before the sexton threw a handful of soil into his grave.

This conversation brought the two beyond the gate and some distance along the avenue, in which the moonlight was somewhat toned by the thickness of the foliage above, and they were rapidly nearing the lodge gates, when suddenly the solemn sound of a deep-toned bell broke the silence. Both men stopped and listened intently.

'That's the passin'-bell,' said Adam. 'Whatever can be up? I never knew it rung at this time of the night before.'

'Make less racket, will you,' said Robin. 'Let's keep count and see how old they are.'

Whilst the bell chimed twenty-six times both listeners stood almost breathless, and then Adam said:

'He's your age, Robin, he is.'

'There was no light in the belfry as we passed by,' said the young man, "I'd rather be in bed than up there working hard at this time, wouldn't you?'

'Yes,' said Adam, 'but old Jemmy doesn't care, and why should he? He's been among the dead too long to be frightened of them night or day, weak and feeble as he is. I dare say he's found out they aren't hard to deal with. There's not much fighting in the burial hole, except perhaps with body snatchers. But let's get home lad, we're likely enough to learn about it in the morning.'

 Without more words they approached the lodge, but to their great terror, when they were within a few yards from the little dwelling, the gates noiselessly swung open, the doleful tolling of the passing-bell being the only sound to be heard. Both men stepped back affrighted as a little figure clad in raiment of a dark hue, but wearing a bright red cap, and chanting some mysterious words in a low musical voice as he walked, stepped into the avenue.

'Stand back, man,' cried Adam, in a terrified voice— 'stand back; it's th' feeorin; but they'll not hurt you if you don't meddle with them.'

The young man forthwith obeyed his aged companion, and standing together against the trunk of a large tree, they gazed at the miniature being stepping so lightly over the road, mottled by the stray moonbeams. It was a dainty little object; but although neither Adam nor Robin could comprehend the burden of the song it sang, the unmistakable croon of grief with which each stave ended told the listeners that the fairy was singing a requiem.

The men kept perfectly silent, and in a little while the figure paused and turned round, as though in expectation, continuing, however, its mournful notes. By-and-by the voices of other singers were distinguished, and as they grew louder the fairy standing in the roadway ceased to render the verse, and sang only the refrain, and a few minutes afterwards Adam and Robin saw a marvellous cavalcade pass through the gateway.

A number of figures, closely resembling the one to which their attention had first been drawn, walked two by two, and behind them others with their caps in their hands, bore a little black coffin, the lid of which was drawn down so as to leave a portion of the contents uncovered. Behind these again others, walking in pairs, completed the procession.

All were singing in inexpressibly mournful tones, pausing at regular intervals to allow the voice of the one in advance to be heard, as it chanted the refrain of the song, and when the last couple had passed into the avenue, the gates closed as noiselessly as they had opened.

As the bearers of the burden marched past the two watchers, Adam bent down, and, by the help of a stray gleam of moonlight, saw that there was a little corpse in the coffin.

'Robin, myi lad,' said he, in a trembling voice and with a scared look, 'it's a double of you that they have in the coffin!'

With a gasp of terror the young man also stooped towards the bearers, and saw clearly enough that the face of the figure borne by the fairies indeed closely resembled his own, save that it was ghastly with the pallor and dews of death.

The procession had passed ere he was able to speak, for, already much affrighted by the appearance of the fairies, the sight of the little corpse had quite unnerved him. Clinging in a terrified manner to the old man, he said, in a broken voice—

'It really was me, Adam! Do you think it's a warning that I'm about to die?'

The old man stepped out into the road as he replied—

'It was a queer sight, Robin, no doubt, but I've seen many such in my time, and they've come to nowt in the end. Warning or not, however,' he added, 'there's no harm done in living as though it was one.'

The mournful music of the strange singers and the solemn sound of the passing bell could still be heard, and the two awe-struck men stood gazing after the cavalcade.

'It must be a warning,' again said Robin, 'I wish I'd asked them how soon I have before I die. Maybe they'd have told me.'

'I don't think they would,' said Adam. 'I've always heard as they're rare and vexed if they're spoken to. They'd probably have done something bad to you if you'd asked anything.'

'They could but have killed me,' replied Robin, adding, with that grim humour which so often accompanies despair, 'and they're burying me now, aren't they?' Then in a calm and firm voice he said—'I'm going to ask them, come what will. If you're frightened, you can go on home.'

'Nay, nay,' said Adam warmly, 'I'm not scared. If you're for asking them, I'll see the end of it.'

Without further parley the men followed after and soon overtook the procession, which was just about to enter the old churchyard, the gates of which, like those of the lodge, swung open apparently of their own accord, and no sooner did Robin come up with the bearers than, in a trembling voice, he cried—

'Will you not tell me how long I've got to live?'

There was not any answer to this appeal, the little figure in front continuing to chant its refrain with even deepened mournfulness. Imagining that he was the leader of the band, Robin stretched out his hand and touched him. No sooner had he done this than, with startling suddenness, the whole cavalcade vanished, the gates banged to with a loud clang, deep darkness fell upon everything, the wind howled and moaned round the church and the tombstones in the graveyard, the branches creaked and groaned overhead, drops of rain pattered upon the leaves, mutterings of thunder were heard, and a lurid flash of lightning quivered down the gloomy avenue.

'I told you how it would be,' said Adam, and Robin simply answered—

'I'm no worse off than before. Let's make towards home, but say nothing to no-one, it would only frighten the women.

Before the two men reached the lodge gates a terrible storm burst over them, and through it they made their way to the distant village.

A great change came over Robin, and from being the foremost in every countryside marlock he became serious and reserved, invariably at the close of the day's work rambling away, as though anxious to shun mankind, or else spending the evening at Adam's talking over 'the warning.' Strange to say, about a month afterwards he fell from a stack, and after lingering some time, during which he often deliriously rambled about the events of the dreadful night, he dozed away, Old Jemmy, the sexton, had another grave to open, and the grey-headed Adam was one of the bearers who carried Robin's corpse along the avenue in which they had so short a time before seen the fairy funeral.

The Chivalrous Devil

About half-a-century ago there lived, in a lane leading away from a little village near Garstang, a poor idiot named Gregory. He was at once the sport and the terror of the young folks. Uniformly kind to them, carefully convoying them to the spots where, in his lonely rambles, he had noticed birds' nests, or pressing upon them the wild flowers he had gathered in the neighbouring woods and thickets, he received at their ungrateful hands all kinds of ill treatment, not always stopping short of personal violence. In this respect, however, the thoughtless children only followed the example set them by their elders, for seldom did poor Gregory pass along the row of cottages, dignified by the name of street, which constituted the village, without an unhandsome head being projected from the blacksmith's or cobbler's shop, or from a doorway, and a cruel taunt being sent after the idiot, who, in his ragged clothing, with his handful of harebells and primroses, and a wreath of green leaves round his battered, old hat, jogged along towards his mother's cottage, singing as he went, in a pathetic monotone, a snatch of an old Lancashire ballad.

In accordance with that holy law which, under such circumstances, influences woman's heart, the mother loved this demented lad with passionate fondness, all the tenderness with which her nature had been endowed having been called forth by the needs of the afflicted child, whose only haven of refuge from the harshness of his surroundings and the cruelty of those who, had not they been as ignorant as the hogs they fed, would have pitied and protected him, was her breast.

Lavishing all her affection upon the poor lad, she had no kindness to spare for those who tormented him; and abstaining from any of those melodramatic and vulgar curses with which a person of less education would have followed those who abused her child, she studiously held herself aloof from her neighbours, and avoided meeting them, except when she was compelled to purchase food or other articles for her little household. This conduct gave an excuse for much ill feeling, and as the woman had no need to toil for her daily bread, and as her cottage was the neatest in the district, there was much jealousy.

One night, at a jovial gathering, it was arranged that a practical joke, of what was considered a very humorous kind, should be played upon the idiot. The boors selected one of their party, whose task it should be to attire himself in a white sheet, and to emerge into the lane when the poor lad should make his appearance. In accordance with this plan the pack of hobbledehoys watched the cottage night after night, in the hope of seeing the idiot leave the dwelling, and at length their patience was rewarded. They immediately hid themselves in the ditch, while the mock ghost concealed himself behind the trunk of a tree.

The lad, not suspecting any evil, came along, humming, in his melancholy monotone, the usual fragment, and just before he reached the tree the sheeted figure slowly stepped forth to the accompaniment of the groanings and bellowings of his associates. They had expected to see the idiot flee in terror; but instead of so doing, he laughed loudly at the white figure, and then suddenly, as the expression of his face changed to one of intense interest, he shouted, 'Oh, oh! a black one! a black one!' Sure enough, a dark and terrible figure stood in the middle of the road. The mock ghost fled, with his companions at his heels, the real spectre chasing them hotly, and the idiot bringing up the rear, shouting at the top of his voice, 'Run, black devil! catch white devil!'

They were not long in reaching the village, down the street of which they ran faster than they ever had run before. Several of them darted into the smithy, where the blacksmith was scattering the sparks right and left as he hammered away at the witch-resisting horseshoes, and others fled into the inn, where they startled the gathered company of idle gossips; but the mock ghost kept on wildly, looking neither to the left nor to the right. The idiot had kept close behind the phantom at the heels of the mock ghost, and when at the end of the village the spectre vanished as suddenly as it had appeared, the lad ran a little faster and took its place. Of this, however, the white-sheeted young fellow was not aware, and, fearing every moment that the shadow would catch him in its awful embrace, he dashed down a by lane. Before he got very far, however, the idiot, who had gradually been lessening the distance between them, overtook and seized him by the neck. With a terrible cry the rustic fell headlong into the ditch, dragging Gregory with him as he fell. The latter was soon upon his feet, and dancing about the lane as he cried, 'Catch white devil! catch white devil!' The mock ghost, however, lay quiet enough among the nettles.

Roused by the story told by the affrighted ones who had rushed so unceremoniously into their presence, as well as by the startling cry of 'Run, black devil! catch white devil!' which the idiot had shouted as he sped past the door, several of the topers emerged from their abiding place; and as nothing could be seen of either mock ghost, spectre, or idiot, they bravely determined to go in search of them. As they passed along the road from the village, their attention was attracted by the cries which seemed to come from the lonely lane, and somewhat nervously making their way along it, they soon saw the idiot dancing about the side of the ditch. With a sudden access of courage, due to the presence of anything human, however weak, they hurried along, and as they drew nearer, the idiot paused in his gambols, and pointed to the mock ghost, who lay stretched in the shadow of the hedgerow. He was soon carried away to the village, where he lay ill for weeks.

The kindness of Gregory's mother to the sick lad's parents, who were very poor and could ill afford to provide the necessary comforts his condition required, caused public feeling to turn in her favour, and those who formerly had been loudest in defaming her became her warmest eulogists. Between the idiot and the young fellow, too, a strange friendship sprang up, and the pair might often be seen passing along the lanes, the idiot chanting his melancholy fragments to the companion whose cap he had adorned with wreaths of wild flowers.

With such a protector the idiot was quite safe, and, indeed, had the village children been wishful to torment Gregory, if the presence of this companion had not sufficed to restrain them, they had only to remember that it was in defence of poor Gregory the Evil One himself had raced through the village.

The Enchanted Fisherman

There are few views in the north of England more
beautiful than that which is seen from Morecambe, as the
spectator looks over the beautiful bay, with its crescent
coast-line of nearly fifty miles in extent. At low water the
dazzling sands, streaked by silvery deceptive channels,
stretch to the distant glimmering sea, the music of whose
heavings comes but faintly on the gentle breeze; but at
tide-time a magnificent expanse of rolling waves sweeps
away to Peel, and is dotted over with red-sailed fishing
boats and coasters. Far to the north the huge heather-
covered Furness Fells stand sentinel-like over the waters,
and above them, dimly seen through the faint blue haze,
tower the grand mountains of the magic lake country.

The scene is full of a sweet dream-like beauty; but there
are times when the beautiful is swallowed in the majestic,
as the mists come creeping over the sea, obscuring the
coasts, and hiding everything save the white caps of the
waves gleaming in the darkness, through which the
muttering diapasons of the wind, as though in deep
distress, sound mysteriously; or when, in winter, the
moon is hidden by scudding clouds, and the huge rollers,
driven before the breeze, dash themselves to death, as
upon the blast come the solemn boom of a signal gun,
and the faint cries of those in danger on the deep.

Years ago, however, before the little village of Poulton
changed its name, and began to dream of becoming a
watering-place, with terraces and hotels, instead of the
picturesque, tumble-down huts of the fishermen, against
which, from time immemorial, the spray had been dashed
by the salt breezes, the only people who gazed upon the
lovely prospect were, with the exception of an occasional

traveller, the families of the toilers of the sea, and the rough-looking men themselves.

These hardy fellows, accustomed to a wild life, and whose days from childhood had been spent on or by the sea, loved the deep with as much tenderness as a strong man feels towards a weak and wayward maiden, for they were familiar with its every mood, with the soothing wash of its wavelets when the sunbeams kissed the foam-bells, as they died on the white sands, and with the noise of the thunder of the breakers chased up the beach by the roaring gales.

One evening a number of these men were seated in the cosy kitchen of the John-o'-Gaunt, listening to 'Owd England' as he narrated some of his strange experiences.

"I remember," said he, "when I was just a young lad, Tom Grisdale being drowned, and now as we're talking about the dangers of the sands, you'll maybe pay attention to this tale.

Poor Tom was the best cockler in Hest Bank, and as used to the sands as a child is to the face of its mother, but for all that he drowned on them after all. I can still remember it well, for young as I was, I was old enough to think about how strange it was, and the sight of the dead bodies at the next low tide was with me day and night for long afterwards.

The day when Tom and his missus and the two lasses set out to see some relations on the missus side, who lived in the Furness country, the old man and the daughters in the cart and the woman riding along at the side. It was a lovely afternoon, at the back end of the year.

The day that they should have come back was very misty, and it was starting to get dark, just as here and there a light was beginning to twinkle in the windows, and the stars to peek out, the noise of a cart crunching over the beach brought my father to the door. "Why, old Tom Grisdale's cart is back again," he cried out. He darted out of the door, with me following after him, as fast as I could. A crowd of folk and children soon gathered round, wondering what was up, but nothing could be learned, for though the lasses were there, looking bright and pretty as a posy of flowers, they were frightened and dazed, and too shocked with wet and cold, to say a word. One thing, however, was sure enough, their old folk hadn't come back, and though the tide had covered their tracks, and was shining in the moonlight, where the mist could shine through that is, a lot of the young cocklers started out searching for them.

The older and more experienced, however, wouldn't hear of it. Two lives in one day was quite enough, they said, so they waited until the tide was going out, and then started, me amongst them, as my father was too distracted talking to the others to send me home.

It was a sad outing, but it was lovely compared to coming back, for when we turned towards Hest Bank, the strongest of the lads carried the bodies of Tom and his missus. We hadn't got far out over the sands before we found the poor old lass, and not far off, in the deep channel, old Tom himself.

They were buried in the old churchyard, and one of the lasses was laid besides them, as she'd died of the fright soon afterwards. When the other sister recovered a bit, and could stand to talk about it, she said that they'd got lost in the mist, and the old man left them on the cart while he walked around a little to find the channel.

When he didn't come back, they got frightened, but the old woman wouldn't stir from the spot until they heard the waters coming, and then they went a short way from the cart, but couldn't find Tom, though they thought they could hear him shouting to them now and then.

The shouts, however, got fainter and fainter, and at last stopped all together. Giving themselves up for lost, they loosened the reins for the mare to find her own way. The poor old lass was quite dazed at the absence of Tom, and as she was swimming across the channel with the cart, she lost her hold and was carried away by the water. The lasses knew no more until they saw the folk running up to the cart upon the beach.

The girl that was left, she was always a bit queer after that, and she used to walk along the bay at the turn of the tide, you know, and it was pitiful to hear her when she'd say she could still hear her old father's voice as he shouted after wandering off from them, and couldn't find his way back to them in the mist.

Later, she went into service in Lancaster, to a place that the parson found for her, with the idea that a change of scenery would do her good. But it wasn't long before the news came that she'd been admitted to the asylum, and I heard that she died soon after that.

No sooner had the grey-headed old fisherman finished his story than one of the auditors said, "You may well fancy she imagined hearing the voice of her father, for many a night and day, but I heard that cry myself. You may stare, but there's more sounds to be heard in the bay than you or most other people know of – and I'm no child to be scared of the dark. Why, only the night before last I heard a peal of bells ringing under the water.

There was a moment of surprise, for Roger Heathcote was not a likely man to be a victim to his own fancies, or to be influenced by the superstitions which clung to his fellows. Like the rest of his companions, he had spent the greatest portion of his life away from land; and either because he possessed keener powers of observation than they, or loved nature more, and therefore watched her more closely, he had gradually added to his store of knowledge, until he had become the recognised authority on all matters connected with the dangerous calling by which the men-folk of the little colony earned daily bread for their families. As he was by no means addicted to yarns, looks of wonder came over the faces of the listeners; and in deference to the wishes of Old England, who pressed him as to what he had heard and seen, Roger narrated the adventure embodied in this story.

The fisherman's little boat was dancing lightly on the rippling waters of the bay.

The night was perfectly calm, the moon shining faintly through a thin mist which rested on the face of the deep. It was nearly midnight, and Roger was thinking of making for home, when he heard the sweet sounds of a peal of bells. Not without astonishment, he endeavoured to ascertain from what quarter the noises came, and, strange and unlikely as it seemed, it appeared that the chimes rang up through the water, upon which, with dreamy motion, his boat was gliding. Bending over the side of the skiff he again heard with singular distinctness the music of the bells pealing in weird beauty.

For some time he remained in this attitude, intently listening to the magical music, and when he arose, the mist had cleared off, and the moon was throwing her lovely light upon the waters, and over the distant fells.

Instead, however, of beholding a coast with every inch of which he was acquainted, Roger gazed upon a district of which he knew nothing. There were mountains, but they were not those whose rugged outlines were so vividly impressed upon his memory. There was a beach, but it was not the one where his little cottage stood with its light in the window and its background of wind-bent trees. The estuary into which his boat was gliding was not that of the Kent, with its ash and oak-covered crags. Everything seemed unreal, even the streaming moonlight having an unusual whiteness, and Roger rapidly hoisted his little sails, but they only flapped idly against the mast, as the boat, in obedience to an invisible and unknown agency, drifted along the mysterious looking river.

As the fisherman gazed in helpless wonder, gradually the water narrowed, and in a short time a cove was gained, the boat grating upon the gleaming sand. Roger at once jumped upon the bank, and no sooner had he done so, than a number of little figures clad in green ran towards him from beneath a clump of trees, the foremost of them singing—

To the home of elf and fay,
To the land of nodding flowers,
To the land of Ever Day
Where all things own the Fay Queen's powers,
Mortal come away!

and the remainder dancing in circles on the grass, and joining in the refrain—

To the home of elf and fay,
To the land of Ever Day,
Mortal come away!

The song finished, the little fellow who had taken the solo, tripped daintily to Roger, and, with a mock bow, grasped one of the fingers of the fisherman's hand, and stepped away as though anxious to lead him from the water.

Assuming that he had come upon a colony of Greenies, and feeling assured that such tiny beings could not injure him, even if anxious to do so, Roger walked on with his conductor, the band dancing in a progressing circle in front of them, until a wood was reached, when the dancers broke up the ring and advanced in single file between the trees.

The light grew more and more dim, and when the cavalcade reached the entrance to a cavern, Roger could hardly discern the Greenies. Clinging to the little hand of his guide, however, the undaunted fisherman entered the cave, and groped his way down a flight of mossy steps. Suddenly he found himself in a beautiful glade, in which hundreds of little figures closely resembling his escort, and wearing dainty red caps, were disporting themselves and singing—

Moonbeams kissing odorous bowers
Light our home amid the flowers;

While our beauteous King and Queen
Watch us dance on rings of green.
Rings of green, rings of green,
Dance, dance, dance, on rings of green.

No sooner had the fisherman entered the glade than the whole party crowded round him, but as they did so a strain of enchanting music was heard, and the little beings hopped away again, and whirled round in a fantastic waltz. Roger himself was so powerfully influenced by the melody that he flung himself into the midst of the dancers, who welcomed him with musical cries, and he capered about until sheer fatigue forced him to sink to rest upon a flowery bank.

Here, after watching for a while the graceful gambols of the Greenies, and soothed by the weird music, the sensuous odours, and the dreamy light, he fell into a deep sleep. When he awoke from his slumber the fairies had vanished, and the fisherman felt very hungry. No sooner, however, had he wished for something to eat than on the ground before him there appeared a goodly array of delicacies, of which, without more ado, Roger partook.

'I'm in luck's way here,' he said to himself; 'It's not every day of the week I see a full table like this. I should like to know where I am, though.' As the wish passed his lips he saw before him a beautiful little being, who said in a sweet low voice—

In the land of nodding flowers,
Where all things own the Fay Queen's powers!

The fisherman no sooner saw the exquisite face of the dainty Greenie than he forgot altogether the rosy-cheeked wife at home, and fell hopelessly over head and heels in love with the sweet vision. Gazing into her beautiful eyes he blurted out, 'I don't care where it is if you are there.'

With a smile the queen, for it was indeed the queen, seated herself at his side. 'Dost thou, Mortal, bow to my power?' asked she. 'Ay, indeed, do I to the forgetfulness of everything but thy bonny face,' answered Roger; upon which the queen burst into a hearty fit of laughter, so musical, however, that for the life of him the fisherman could not feel angry with her. 'If the king were to hear thee talking thus thou wouldst pay dearly for thy presumption,' said the Fay, as she rose and tripped away to the shadow of the trees. The enraptured Roger endeavoured to overtake her before she reached the oaks, but without success; and though he wandered through the wood for hours, he did not again catch a glimpse of her. He gained an appetite by the freak however, and no sooner had he wished for food again than dishes of rich viands appeared before him.

'I wish I could get money at this rate,' said the fisherman, and the words had hardly left his lips when piles of gold ranged themselves within his reach. Roger rapidly filled his pockets with the glittering coins, and even took the shoes from off his feet, and filled them also, and then slung them round his neck by the strings.

'Now, if I could but get to my boat,' thought he, 'my fortune would be made,' and accordingly he began to make his way in what he believed to be the direction of the river. He had not proceeded very far, however, when he emerged upon an open space surrounded by tall foxgloves, in all the beautiful bells of which dreamy-eyed little beings were swinging lazily as the quiet zephyr rocked their perfumed dwellings.

Some of the Greenies were quite baby fairies not so large as Roger's hand, but none of them seemed alarmed at the presence of a mortal. A score of larger ones were hard at work upon the sward stitching together moth and butterfly wings for a cloak for their Queen, who, seated upon a mushroom, was smiling approvingly as she witnessed the industry of her subjects. Roger felt a sudden pang as he observed her, for although he was glad once more to behold the marvellous beauty of her face, he was jealous of a dainty dwarf in a burnished suit of beetles' wing cases and with a fantastic peaked cap in which a red feather was coquettishly stuck, for this personage he suspected was the King, and forgetting his desire to escape with the gold, and at once yielding to his feelings, he flung himself on the luxuriant grass near the little being whose weird loveliness had thrown so strange a glamour over him, and without any thought or fear as to the consequences he at once bent himself and kissed one of her dainty sandalled feet.

No sooner had he performed this rash act of devotion than numberless blows fell upon him from all sides, but he was unable to see any of the beings by whom he was struck. Instinctively the fisherman flung his huge fists about wildly, but without hitting any of the invisible Greenies, whose tantalising blows continued to fall upon him. At length, however, wearying of the fruitless contest, he roared out, 'I wish I were safe in my boat in the bay,' and almost instantaneously he found himself in the little skiff, which was stranded high and dry upon the Poulton beach.

The shoes which he had so recently filled with glittering pieces of gold and suspended round his neck were again upon his feet, his pockets were as empty as they were when he had put out to sea some hours before, and somewhat dubious and very disgusted, in a few minutes he had crept off to bed.

When the strange tale of the fisherman's wonderful adventure with the hill folk was ended, the unbelievers did not hesitate to insinuate that Roger had not been out in the bay at all, and that the land of nodding flowers might be found by anyone who stayed as long and chalked up as large a score at the John-o'-Gaunt as he had done on the night when he heard the submerged bells and had so unusual a catch.

Others, however, being less sceptical, many were the little boats that afterwards went on unsuccessful voyages in search of the mysterious estuary and the colony of Greenies, and a year afterwards, when a sudden gale swept over the restless face of the deep and cast Roger's boat bottom upwards upon the sandy beach, many believed that the fisherman had again found the land of Ever Day.

The Sands of Cocker

The quiet little village of Cockerham is hardly the spot one would expect to find selected as a place of residence by a gentleman of decidedly fast habits, and to whom a latch-key is indispensable; yet once upon a time the Evil One himself, it is said, took up his quarters in the go-to-bed-early hamlet.

It hardly need be stated that the undesirable resident caused no small stir in the hitherto drowsy little place. Night after night he prowled about with clanking chains, and shed an unpleasantly-suggestive odour of sulphur, that rose to the diamond-paned windows and crept through cracks and chinks to the nasal organs of the horrified villagers, who had been disturbed by the ringing of the Satanic bracelets, and, fearing to sleep whilst there was so strong a smell of brimstone about, lay awake, thinking of the sins they had committed, or intended to commit if they escaped 'Old Skrat.'

Before the wandering perfumer had thus, above a score of times, gratuitously fumigated the villagers, a number of the more daring ones, whose courage rose when they found that after all they were not flown away with, resolved that they would have a meeting, at which the unjustifiable conduct of a certain individual should be discussed, and means be devised of ridding the village of his odoriferous presence. In accordance with this determination, a gathering was announced for noonday, for the promoters of the movement did not dare to assemble after sunset to discuss such a subject. After a few cursory remarks from the chairman, and a long and desultory discussion as to the best way of getting rid of the self-appointed night watchman, it was settled that the schoolmaster, as the most learned man in the place, should be the deputation, and have all the honour and profit of an interview with the nocturnal rambler.

Strange as it may appear, the pedagogue was nothing loath to accept the office, for if there was one thing more than another for which he had longed, it was an opportunity of immortalising himself; the daily round of life in the village certainly affording but few chances of winning deathless fame. He therefore at once agreed to take all the risks if he might also have all the glory. Not that he purposed to go to the Devil; no, the mountain should come to Mahomet; the Evil One should have the trouble of coming to him.

His determination was loudly applauded by the assembled villagers, each of whom congratulated himself upon an escape from the dangerous, if noble, task of ridding the place of an intolerable nuisance.

There was no time to be lost, and a night or two afterwards, no sooner had the clock struck twelve, than the schoolmaster, who held a branch of ash and a bunch of vervain in his hand, chalked the conventional circle upon the floor of his dwelling, stepped within it, and in a trembling voice began to repeat the Lord's Prayer backwards. When he had muttered about half of the spell thunder began to roar in the distance; rain splashed on the roof, and ran in streams from the eaves; a gust of wind moaned round the house, rattling the loose leaded panes, shaking the doors, and scattering the embers upon the hearth. At the same time the solitary light, which had begun to burn a pale and ghastly blue, was suddenly extinguished, as though by an invisible hand; but the terrified schoolmaster was not long left in darkness, for a vivid flash of lightning illuminated the little chamber, and almost blinded the would-be necromancer, who tried to gabble a prayer in the orthodox manner, but his tongue refused to perform its office, and clave to the roof of his mouth.

At that moment, could he have made his escape, he would willingly have given to the first comer all the glory he had panted to achieve; but even had he dared to leave the magic circle, there was not time to do so, for almost immediately there was a second blast of wind, before which the trees bent like blades of grass, a second flash lighted up the room, a terrible crash of thunder shook the house to its foundations, and, as a number of evil birds, uttering doleful cries, dashed themselves through the window, the door burst open, and the schoolmaster felt that he was no longer alone.

An instantaneous silence, dreadful by reason of the contrast, followed, and the moon peeped out between the driving clouds and threw its light into the chamber. The birds perched themselves upon the window sill and ceased to cry, and with fiery-looking eyes peered into the room, and suddenly the trembling amateur saw the face of the dark gentleman whose presence only a few minutes before he had so eagerly desired.

Overpowered by the sight, his knees refused to bear him up, what little hair had not been removed from his head by the stupidity of the rising generation stood on end, and with a miserable groan he sank upon his hands and knees, but, fortunately for himself, within the magic ring, round which the Evil One was running rapidly. How long this gratuitous gymnastic entertainment continued he knew not, for he was not in a state of mind to judge of the duration of time, but it seemed an age to the unwilling observer, who, afraid of having the Devil behind him, and yielding to a mysterious mesmeric influence, endeavoured, by crawling round backward, to keep the enemy's face in front. At length, however, the saltatory fiend asked in a shrill and unpleasant voice,

'Rash fool, what wantest thou with me? Couldst thou not wait until in the ultimate and proper course of things we had met?'

Terrified beyond measure not only at the nature of the pertinent question, but also by the insinuation and the piercing and horrible tone in which it was spoken, the tenant of the circle knew not what reply to make, and merely stammered and stuttered—

'Good Old Nick, go away for ever, and'—

'Take thee with me,' interrupted the Satanic one quickly. 'Even so; such is my intent.'

Upon this the poor wretch cried aloud in terror, and again the Evil One began to hop round and round and round the ring, evidently in the hope of catching a part of the body of the occupant projecting over the chalk mark.

'Is there no escape,' plaintively asked the victim in his extremity, 'is there no escape?'

Upon this Old Nick suddenly stopped his gambols and quietly said,

'Three chances of escape shalt thou have, but if thou failest, then there is no appeal. Set me three tasks, and if I cannot perform any one of them, then art thou free.'

There was a glimmer of hope in this, and the shivering necromancer brightened up a little, actually rising from his ignoble position and once more standing erect, as he gleefully said,

'I agree.'

'Ah, ah,' said the Evil One *sotto voce*.

'Count the raindrops on the hedgerows from here to Ellel,' cried the schoolmaster.

'Thirteen,' immediately answered Satan, 'the wind I raised when I came shook all the others off.'

'One chance gone,' said the wizard, whose knees again began to manifest signs of weakness.

There was a short pause, the schoolmaster evidently taking time to consider, for, after all, life, even in a place like Cockerham, was sweet in comparison with what might be expected in the society of the odoriferous one whose mirth was so decidedly ill-timed and unmusical. The silence was not of long continuance, however, for the Evil One began to fear that a detestably early cock might crow, and thereby rescue the trembling one from his clutches. In his impatience, therefore, he knocked upon the floor with his cloven hoof and whistled loudly, after the manner followed now-a-days by dirty little patrons of the drama, perched high in the gallery of a twopenny theatre, and again danced rapidly round the ring in what the tenant deemed unnecessary proximity to the chalk mark.

'Count the ears of corn in old Tithepig's field,' suddenly cried the schoolmaster.

'Three millions and twenty-six,' at once answered Satan.

'I have no way of checking it,' moaned the pedagogue.

'Ah, ah,' bellowed the fiend, who now, instead of hopping round the ring, capered in high glee about the chamber.

'Ho, ho!' laughed the schoolmaster, 'I have it! Here it is! Ho, ho! Twist a rope of sand and wash it in the river Cocker without losing a grain.'

The Evil One stepped out of the house, to the great relief of its occupier, who at once felt that the atmosphere was purer; but in a few minutes he returned with the required rope of sand.

'Come along,' said he, 'and see it washed.' And he swung it over his shoulder, and stepped into the lane.

In the excitement of the moment the wizard had almost involuntarily stepped out of the magic circle, when suddenly he bethought himself of the danger, and drily said—

'Thank you; I'll wait here. By the light of the moon I can see you wash it.'

The baffled fiend, without more ado, stepped across to the rippling streamlet, and dipped the rope into the water, but when he drew it out he gave utterance to a shout of rage and disappointment, for half of it had been washed away.

'Hurrah!' shouted the schoolmaster. 'Cockerham against the world!' And as in his joy he jumped out of the ring, the Evil One, instead of seizing him, in one stride crossed Pilling Moss and Broadfleet, and vanished, and from that night to the present day Cockerham has been quite free from Satanic visits.

The Silver Token

Believe in Fairies? 'Aye, that I do, though I never clapped my eyes on 'em,' said old Nancy to a group of gaping listeners seated by the farm-house kitchen fire.

'That's queer' remarked a sceptical young woman in the ingle nook.

Old Nancy gave her a scornful glance, and then went on:

'I never saw a fairy as far as I know, but I used to serve one on 'em with milk. You might stare; but the way of it were this... I was at my work in the dairy one day, about when it was getting dark, when all of a sudden a little jug clapped itself down in front of me on the stone. You may be sure I was confused, for where it came from, or how it got there, I couldn't make out.

I bent myself down to get hold of it, and it was like it was made of silver, it was that bright and shiny, but it was as light as a feather, and I couldn't tell what it was made of. I bent to set it on the stone again, when I saw a new sixpenny bit had been put there with it, so it struck me that it was milk that was wanted.

So I filled the jug, set in down again, and as soon as I'd put it where I'd got it from, it was up and whipped out of sight. Well, I thought it mightily queer, but I'd heard my father say, many and many a time, as those that get fairy brass given to them should tell nobody, so I kept it to myself, though it was hard work to, you can be sure.

Every night the jug and the sixpenny bit clapped themselves on the stone as regular as milking time, and I filled the jug and picked up the brass.

At last, however, I thought that no harm would come of it if I only told one person, so when Roger there and me got engaged to be married, I told him what sort of a nest egg I'd been getting so strangely. My father was right, however, for the next night neither jug nor sixpenny bit turned up, and from that day to this I've seen no more of them, and it's over forty years since I picked up the last coin.'

The Headless Woman[3]

It was near upon twelve when Gabriel Fisher bade good night to the assembled roysterers who were singing and shouting in the kitchen of the White Bull, at Longridge, and, turning his back to the cosy hearth, upon which a huge log was burning, emerged into the moonlit road.

With his dog Trotty close at his heels, he struck out manfully towards Tootal Height and Thornley, for he had a long and lonely walk before him. It was a clear and frosty night, but occasionally a light cloud sailed across the heavens, and obscured the moon. Rapidly passing between the two rows of cottages which constituted the little straggling village, his footsteps ringing upon the frozen ground, Gabriel made for the fells, and, as he hurried along, he hummed to himself a line of the last song he had heard, and now and again burst into a fit of laughter as he remembered a humorous story told by 'Owd Shuffler.'

When he reached the highest point of the road whence he could see the beautiful Chipping valley, a soft breeze was whispering among the fir-trees, with that faint rustle suggestive of the gentle fall of waves upon a beach. Here and there a little white farm-house or labourer's cottage was gleaming in the moonlight, but the inmates had been asleep for hours.

There was an air of loneliness and mystery over everything; and though Gabriel would have scorned to

---

[3] "Beawt Heeod" in the original text

admit that he was afraid of anything living or dead, before he had passed out of the shadow of the weird-looking melodious branches he found himself wishing for other company than that of his dog. He suddenly remembered, too, with no access of pleasurable feelings, that on the previous day he had seen a solitary magpie, and all sorts of stories of 'Banister Dolls' and 'Jinny Greenteeths,' with which his youthful soul had been carefully harrowed, came across his mind. He tried to laugh at these recollections, but the attempt was by no means a successful one, and he gave expression to a hearty wish that Kemple End were not quite so far off.

Just then a sharp shrill cry fell upon his ear, and then another and another. 'The Gabriel Ratchets,' he shouted, 'what's about to happen?' The cries were not repeated, however, and he went on, but when he reached the peak of the fell, and gazed before him into the deep shade of a plantation, he could not repress a slight shudder, for he fancied that he saw something moving at a distance. He paused for a moment or two to assure himself, and then went on again slowly, his heart throbbing violently as he lessened the space between the moving object and himself. The dog, as though equally influenced by similar feelings, crept behind him in a suspicious and terrified manner.

'It's nobbut a woman,' said he, somewhat re-assured; 'it's a woman surely. Maybe somebody's ill, and she's going for help. Come on, Trotty, man.'

So saying, he quickened his pace, the dog hanging behind, until he approached almost close to the figure, when, with a wild howl, away Trotty fled down the hillside. As Gabriel drew still closer, he saw that the object wore a long light cloak and hood, and a large coal-scuttle bonnet; and surprised to find that the sound of his footsteps did not cause her to turn to see who was following, he called out:

'It's a bonny night, Missus; but you're out rather late, aren't you?'

'It is very fine,' answered the woman, in a voice which Gabriel thought was the sweetest he had ever heard, but without turning towards him as she spoke.

'Something wrong at your folk's, happen?' he asked, anxious to prolong the talk. There was no reply to this, though, and Gabriel knew not what to think, for the silent dame, although she declined to reply, continued to keep pace with him, and to walk at his side.

Was it someone who had no business to be out at that hour, and who did not wish to be recognised, he wondered? But if so, thought he, why did she continue to march in a line with him? The voice, certainly, was that of one of a different rank to his own; but, on the other hand, he reflected, if she were one of the gentle folks, why the cottager's cloak and bonnet, and the huge market basket? These conjectures crossed his brain in rapid succession; and influenced by the last one—that as to his companion's clothing—he determined again to address her.

'You might have left your tongue at home, Missus,' said he, 'since you cannot answer a civil man.'

This taunt, however, like the direct query, failed to provoke an answer, although the startled Gabriel could have sworn that a smothered laugh came from beneath the white cloth which covered the contents of the basket 'Let me carry your basket,' said he; 'it's heavy for you'.'

Without a word, the woman held it out to him; but, as Gabriel grasped the handle, a voice, which sounded as though the mouth of the speaker were close to his hand, slowly said:

'You're very kind, I'm sure;' and then there came from the same quarter a silvery peal of laughter.

'What in the world can it be?' said Gabriel, as without more ado he let the basket fall to the ground. He did not remain in ignorance very long, however, for, as the white cloth slipped off, a human head, with fixed eyes, rolled out 'The headless boggart!' cried he, as the figure turned to pick up the head, and revealed to him an empty bonnet, and away he fled down the hill, fear lending him speed. He had not run far, however, before he heard a clatter of feet on the hard road behind him; but Gabriel was one of the fleetest lads about the fells, and the sight he had just seen was calculated to bring out all his powers; so the sound did not grow louder, but just as he turned into the old Chaighley Road, the head, thrown by the boggart, came whizzing past in unpleasant proximity to his own, and went rolling along in front of him.

For a second or two Gabriel hesitated what to do, the headless woman behind and the equally terrible head in front; but it did not take long to decide, and he went forward with renewed vigour, thinking to pass the dreadful thing rapidly rolling along in advance of him. No sooner was he near to it, however, than, with an impish laugh, which rang in his ears for days afterwards, the ghastly object diverged from its course and rolled in his way. With a sudden and instinctive bound, he leaped over it; and as he did so the head jumped from the ground and snapped at his feet, the teeth striking together with a dreadfully suggestive clash. Gabriel was too quick for it, however, but for some distance he heard with horrible distinctness the clattering of the woman's feet and the banging of the head upon the road behind him.

Gradually the sounds grew fainter as he speeded along, and at length, after he had crossed a little stream of water which trickled across the lane from a fern-covered spring in the fell side, the sounds ceased altogether. The runner, however, did not pause to take breath until he had reached his home and had crept beneath the blankets, the trembling Trotty, whom he found crouched in terror at the door of the cottage, skulking upstairs at his heels and taking refuge under the bed.

'I always said as you'd be seeing a feeorin with all your stopping out at night,' remarked his spouse after he had narrated his adventure; 'but if it does nothing else buy makes you pay more time across your own threshold, I'd be glad of it, for its more than a woman with a head ON her shoulders has been able to do.'

The Rescue of Moonbeam

From one corner of Ribbleton Moor, the scene of
Cromwell's victory over Langdale, there is as lovely a
view as ever painter dreamed of. Far below the spectator
the Ribble sweeps almost in a circle beneath the scars
which, by the action of years of this washing, have been
scooped out so as to form a large precipice, under which
the waters flow, marking out in their course the great
'horse-shoe meadow,' with its fringe of shining sand. The
peaceful valley through which the river, reflecting in its
moving bosom the overhanging many-tinted woods and
cliffs, meanders on its way to the sea, is bounded afar-off
by noble hills, the whale-like Pendle towering in majestic
grandeur above the rest. From the moor a rough and
stony lane winds down the wooded hillside, past a
beautiful old half-timbered house down to the dusty
highway and the bridge over the Belisamia of the
Romans. The beautiful river, with its tremulous earth and
sky pictures, the meadows and corn-fields whence come
now and again the laugh and song of the red-faced
mowers and reapers, the clearly-defined roads and white
farm-houses, the spires of distant hillside churches, and
the rich green of the waving woods, make up an
enchanting picture.

When night comes, however, and the lovely stars peep
out, and the crescent moon casts her glamour over the
dreaming earth, and half-hidden in a dimly transparent
veil of shimmering mist the Ribble glides as gently as
though it had paused to listen to its own melody, a still
deeper loveliness falls upon the dreaming landscape, over
which the very genius of beauty seems to hover silently
with outspread wings.

At such a time, when moon and stars threw a faint and mysterious light over the sleeping woods, and not a sound, save the cry of a restless bird, broke the silence, a young countryman made his way rapidly across the horse-shoe meadow to the bend of the stream under Red Scar.

It was not to admire the beautiful scenery, however, that Reuben Oswaldwistle was crossing the dew-besprinkled field, over which faint odours of hay were wafted by a gentle breeze. The sturdy young fellow was too practical to yield entirely to such an influence, and although he was by no means unlearned in the traditions and stories of the neighbourhood, long familiarity had taught him to look upon the landscape with the eye of a farmer. He was simply about to practise the gentle art in the hope of beguiling a few stray 'snigs' for dinner on the following day.

Still the scene in all its glamour of moonlight and peace was not powerless even upon his rude nature; so, after setting his lines, he took out a little black pipe, filled it from a capacious moleskin pouch, and after lighting the fragrant weed, gave way to a train of disconnected fancies—past, present, and future mingling strangely in his reverie.

What with the rustling of the leaves overhead, the musical rippling of the river as it danced over the stones on its way to the sea, and the soothing effect of the tobacco, Reuben was beginning to doze, when suddenly he fancied he heard the sound of a light footstep in the grass behind him. Turning round somewhat drowsily, he beheld a little figure of about a span high, clad in green, and wearing a dainty red cap, struggling along under the load of a flat-topped mushroom much larger than itself. After having more than once fallen with its load, the dwarf cried out in a sweet, faint voice, 'Dewdrop, Dewdrop!' and no sooner had the sound died into silence than another little who evidently answered to the pretty name, came tripping from the shadow of a hawthorn.

'What's the matter, Moonbeam?' said the new-comer, cheerily.

'This table is too much for me,' answered the labourer whom Reuben had seen first, 'and if the king's dinner is not ready to a minute he will have me stung. Help me with this load, there's a good sort.'

Without any more ado Dewdrop came forward and the tiny pair put their shoulders beneath the load and marched off. They did not bear it very far, however, for the astonished Reuben simply stretched himself at full length on the grass and again was quite close to them.

The two dots stopped when they came to a hole, into which they at once stuck the stem of the mushroom. Moonbeam then took from his pocket a butterfly's wing, which served him as a handkerchief, and wiping his forehead as he spoke, he said:—

'I'm about tired of this. Every night the table is stolen, Dewdrop, and I've to find a new one for each dinner, and no thanks for it either. What has come of late over the king I am at a loss to imagine, for he has done nothing but have me stung. I shall emigrate if this continues, that's all.'

'So would I,' answered the other little fellow, 'if Blue-eyes would go also, but I can't leave her.'

After a hearty peal of laughter, during which he had held his shaking sides, Moonbeam shouted—

'Why, my dear innocent, if you went she would be after you in a trice. I remember that when I was as guileless as you I fell in love with Ravenhair, the daughter of old Pigear. She treated me just as Blue-eyes uses you, but when, in a fit of jealous rage, I began to pay delicate attentions to Jasmine, the tables soon were turned, and one evening, as I was dozing in a flower cup, I heard someone call me, and peeping out of my chamber, I saw the once scornful Ravenhair weeping at the foot of the stalk. No sooner did she catch a glimpse of the tip of my nightcap than in piteous tones, that went straight to my heart, she cried out, "Dearest Moony, let me come up and"—. But, hush! wasn't that the dinner gong?'

The pair listened intently as over the grass came the solemn hum of a bee.

'I'm in for it,' said the fairy whose tale had been so suddenly interrupted; 'there's the first bell, and I haven't got even the table set.'

The pair darted off, and tripping away into the shade of the hawthorn, they were for a moment or two lost to the sight of the wondering Reuben, but they soon returned, each bearing a dish and cover made of a little pearl shell. These they placed upon the mushroom, and away they scudded, again to return in a minute with another load. In an incredibly short space of time the table was set out with a goodly array of tiny dishes and plates.

Once more the hum of the bee was heard booming over the grass, and from the shadow of the tree there emerged a dainty being whose attire glittered in the moonlight, and whose step was like that of a proud monarch. He was clad in a many-hued coat made of wings of dragon flies, a green vest cut from a downy mouse-ear leaf, and with buttons of buttercup buds; little knee-breeches of fine-spun silk dyed in the juice of a whinberry, stockings of cobweb, and shoes of shining beetle case; his shirt, which

was as white as falling snow, had been cut from
convolvulus flowers ere they had opened to the light; and
his hat, a gem of a thing fit only for a fairy, was of red
poppy, with a waving white feather, and a band of fur
from a caterpillar. He led by the hand another personage,
equally daintily dressed, but of a higher order of
loveliness, with a pale oval face, and dreamy-looking eyes,
gleaming like the sea when the moon and stars are
bending over its bosom, and the wind is whispering its
sad secrets. Her hair was golden, and rippled almost to
her exquisite feet, and over it she wore a blue cornflower
wreath, with diamond dewdrops here and there amid the
leaves. Her dress was of damask rose leaves looped up
with myosotis.

The grass hardly bent beneath her, so daintily did she trip
along, just touching the tips of the fingers of the hand the
king extended to her. Following this royal pair came a
group of gaily-clad attendants, and a band discoursing
sweet sounds, the deep bass of bees harmonising happily
with the barytone of a beetle and the crescendo chirp of a
cricket.

With a loud flourish from the musicians all took their
places at the festive mushroom, and the banquet began.
The dishes were sufficiently various to tempt even an
anchorite to excess, for all the delicacies of the season
were there. Ladybird soup, baked stickleback, roasted leg
of nightingale, boiled shoulder of frog with cranberry
sauce, wild strawberry tarts, and numerous kinds of fruits
and juices, made up a dainty repast, of which king, queen,
and courtiers partook heartily. The band, the members of
which were perched in the swinging flowers of a foxglove
close by, played lustily during the feast.

'For once,' said the king, 'for once—and let the
circumstance be remembered when the annals of our

reign are written—a day hath passed without anything having annoyed our royal self, without anything unpleasant having happened in our royal presence, and without anything having disagreed with our royal stomach.'

No sooner had these words passed the royal lips, however, than the queen gave a faint shriek, and cried out—

'My love, there is not a drop of my chickweed wine on the table.'

A dark cloud passed over the monarch's face as he angrily shouted—

'Methinks we were congratulating our royal self somewhat too early in the day. Bring hither the rascally Moonbeam and bid the executioners attend for orders.'

One of the courtiers, with an alacrity marvellously resembling that of beings of a larger growth, rushed out, and speedily returned with the unfortunate dependant, who at once flung himself on the ground before the angry king and begged to be forgiven. What result might have followed these prayers is uncertain, for, unfortunately, the suppliant's tears fell upon one of the monarch's shoes and dimmed its lustre.

'Bring hither the executioners and their instruments,' roared the infuriated king, and almost immediately a couple of sturdy little fellows appeared leading by a chain two large wasps.

'Do your disreputable work!' shouted the monarch.

The executioners seized Moonbeam, fastened him to a stake, and pressed a wasp against him. The insect instantly stung him, and the miserable little fellow howled with pain.

'Take him away,' cried the queen; 'we don't want *whine* of that kind.'

'What a wretched pun!' involuntarily said Moonbeam, as they were dragging him from the royal presence.

'Bring the villain back,' roared the King; 'bring him back, and sting him until he is less critical.'

'If tha hez him stung ageeon,' interrupted the indignant Reuben, who in his excitement had gradually crept nearer to the royal table, 'I'll knock thi proud little heeod off, chuz who tha art.'

Neither the king or the executioners, however, took the slightest notice of the warning, so, as the latter were once more forcing the unhappy Moonbeam against the other wasp, down came a huge fist upon the royal head.

'Theer,' said the fisherman, exultingly, 'I towd tha, didn't I, bud tha wouldn't tek wernin'. Tha 'rt on 't' penitent form bi this time, I daat.'

Lifting up his hand, however, what was the surprise of the wondering Reuben to find only a little crushed grass under it. King, Queen, courtiers, Moonbeam, executioners, and wasps, all had vanished, and even the band, whose humming and droning he had heard so distinctly during the whole banquet, no longer broke the silence.

'Well,' said the fisherman, 'that's a capper, in o mi born days. I see 'em as plain as a pikestaff. Th' last day connot be far off, I'm sewer. Bud I'll hev th' tabble, at onny rate, beawt axin.' And, so saying, he took possession of the huge mushroom, and after hurriedly gathering up his lines, he wended his way across the meadow to his little cottage by the high road, and arrived there, he narrated to his drowsy wife the story of the banquet.

'Drat th' fairies, an' thee, too, wi' thi gawmless tales,' said his sceptical helpmate, 'I wondered what hed getten tha. Tha's bin asleep for hours i' th' meadow istid a lookin' after th' fish. Tha never seed a fairy i' thi life. Tha'rt nod hauve sharp enough, clivver as tha art i' owt as is awkurt.' There was a short pause after this sally, and then the sly Reuben drily answered—

'Yoy, I 've sin a fairy monny an' monny a time. Olus when I used to come a cooartin' to thi moather's. Bud tha 'r nod mich like a fairy neaw, tha 'st autert terbly. Tha 'rt too thrivin' lookin'.'

'Be off wi' thi fawseness,' said the pleased woman; 'tha 'd ollus a desayvin tung i' thi heead;' and then after a drowsy pause as she was dosing to sleep; 'but for o that I'll mek a soop o' good catsup out o' thi fairy tabble.'

The White Dobbie

Many years ago, long before the lovely Furness district was invaded by the genius of steam, the villagers along the coast from Bardsea to Rampside were haunted by a wandering being whose errand, the purpose of which could never be learned, used to bring him at night along the lonely roads and past the straggling cottages.

This pilgrim was a wearied, emaciated-looking man, on whose worn and wan face the sorrows of life had left deep traces, and in whose feverish, hungry-looking eyes, mystery and terror seemed to lurk. Nobody knew the order of his coming or going, for he neither addressed anyone, nor replied if spoken to, but disregarded alike the 'good neet' of the tramp who knew him not, and the startled cry of the belated villager who came suddenly upon him at a turn of the road. Never stopping even for a minute to gaze through the panes whence streamed the ruddy glow of the wood fires, and to envy the dwellers in the cosy cottages, he kept on his way, as though his mission was one of life and death, and, therefore, would not brook delay.

On wild wintry nights, however, when the salt wind whirled the foam across the bay, and dashed the blinding snow into heaps upon the window-sills and against the cottage doors, and darkness and storm spread their sombre wings over the coast, then was it certain that the mysterious being would be seen, for observation had taught the villagers and the dwellers in solitary houses along the lonely roads between the fishing hamlets that in storm and darkness the weird voyager was most likely to appear.

At such times, when the sound of footsteps, muffled by the snow, was heard between the soughs and moans of the wailing wind, the women cried, 'Heaven save us; 'tis th' White Dobbie,' as, convulsively clutching their little ones closer to their broad bosoms, they crept nearer to the blazing log upon the hearth, and gazed furtively and nervously at the little diamond-paned window, past which the restless wanderer was making his way, his companion running along a little way in advance, for not of the mysterious man alone were the honest people afraid. In front of him there invariably ran a ghastly-looking, scraggy white hare, with bloodshot eyes. No sooner however did anyone look at this spectral animal than it fled to the wanderer, and jumping into his capacious pocket, was lost to sight.

Verily of an unearthly stock was this white hare, for upon its approach and long before it neared a village, the chained dogs, by some strange instinct conscious of its coming, trembled in terror, and frantically endeavoured to snap their bonds; unfastened ones fled no man knew whither; and if one happened to be trotting alongside its belated master as he trudged homeward and chanced to meet the ghastly Dobbie with its blood-red eyes, with a scream of pain almost human in its keen intensity, away home scampered the terrified animal, madly dashing over hedge and ditch as though bewitched and fiend-chased.

For many years the lonely wanderer had traversed the roads, and for many years had the hare trotted in front of him; lads who were cradled upon their mother's knee when first they heard the awe-inspiring footfalls had grown up into hearty wide-chested men, and men who were ruddy fishers when the pilgrim first startled the dwellers in Furness had long passed away into the silent land; but none of them ever had known the wayfarer to utter a syllable. At length, however, the time came when the solemn silence was to be broken.

One night when the breeze, tired of whispering its weird messages to the bare branches, and chasing the withered leaves along the lanes, had begun to moan a hushed prelude to the music of a storm, through the mist that had crept over the bay, and which obscured even the white-crested wavelets at the foot of the hill on which stood the sacred old church, there came at measured intervals the melancholy monotone of the Bardsea passing bell for the dead.

Dismally upon the ears of the dwellers in the straggling hamlet fell the announcement of the presence of death, and even the woman who had for years been bell-ringer and sexton, felt a thrill of fear as she stood in the tower but dimly lighted by a candle in a horn lantern, and high above her head the message of warning rang out; for, although accustomed to the task, it was not often that her services were required at night. Now and again she gazed slowly round the chamber, upon the mouldering walls of which fantastic shadows danced, and she muttered broken fragments of prayers in a loud and terrified voice, for as the door had been closed in order that the feeble light in the lantern might not be extinguished by the gusts of wind, isolated as she was from the little world upon the hillside, she felt in an unwonted manner the utter loneliness of the place and its dread surroundings.

Suddenly she uttered a shrill shriek, for she heard a hissing whisper at her ear and felt an icy breath upon her cheek. She dared not turn round, for she saw that the door opening upon the churchyard remained closed as before, and that occasionally passing within the range of her fixed stare, a white hare with blood-red eyes gambolled round the belfry.

'T' Dobbie!' sighed she, as the dim light began to flicker and the hare suddenly vanished.

As she stood almost paralysed, again came the terrible whisper, and this time she heard the question—

'Who for this time?'

The horrified woman was unable to answer, and yet powerless to resist the strange fascination which forced her to follow the direction of the sound; and when the question was put a second time, in an agony of fear she gazed into the wild eyes of the being at her elbow, her parched tongue cleaving to her open mouth. From the pocket of the dread visitor the ghastly animal gazed at the ringer, who mechanically jerked the bell-rope, and the poor woman was fast losing her senses, when suddenly the door was burst open, and a couple of villagers, who had been alarmed by the irregular ringing, entered the tower. They at once started back as they saw the strange group—the wanderer with sad, inquiring look, and pallid face, the phantom hare with its firelit eyes, and the old ringer standing as though in a trance. No sooner, however, did one of the intruders gaze at the animal than it slipped out of sight down into the pocket of its companion and keeper, and the wanderer himself hastily glided between the astonished men, and out into the darkness of the graveyard.

On many other gloomy nights afterwards the ringer was accosted in the same manner, but although the unnatural being and the spectral hare continued for some winters to pass from village to village and from graveyard to graveyard, a thick cloud of mystery always hung over and about them, and no one ever knew what terrible sin the never-resting man had been doomed to expiate by so lonely and lasting a pilgrimage.

Whence he came and whither he went remained unknown; but long as he continued to patrol the coast the hollow sound of his hasty footsteps never lost its terror to the cottagers; and even after years had passed over without the usual visits, allusions to the weird pilgrim and his dread companion failed not to cause a shudder, for it was believed that the hare was the spirit of a basely-murdered friend, and that the restless voyager was the miserable assassin doomed to a wearisome, lifelong wandering.

The Little Man's Gift

Many are the wells in Lancashire that once were supposed to be the homes of good or evil spirits—of demons or of beneficent fairies—and, despite the injunctions of the Church against the customs of praying at and waking wells, down to a comparatively recent period they were resorted to by pilgrims of all grades who were in search of health. One such spring near Blackpool, known as the Fairies' Well, had its daily crowds of the ailing and the sorrowful, for its water was credited with virtues as wonderful as they were manifold, and from far and near people brought vessels to be filled with the miraculous fluid.

One day at noon, a poor woman who had journeyed many a weary mile in order to obtain a supply of the water with which to bathe the eyes of her child, whose sight was fast failing, and upon whom all the usual remedies had been tried without success, on rising from her knees at the well side, was surprised to find standing near her a handsome little man clad in green, who certainly was not in sight when she bent to fill her bottle.

As she stood gazing at the dainty object, the visitor, without having previously asked her any questions, handed to her a beautiful box filled with ointment, and directed her to apply the salve to the eyes of her child, whose sight it would restore. Surprised beyond measure at the little man's knowledge of her family affairs, the woman mechanically accepted the gift, but when, after carefully placing the box in her pocket, she turned to thank the giver, he was no longer to be seen; and satisfied that she had had an interview with one of the beings after whom the well was named, she started on her journey to her distant home.

The strangeness of the present, given as she trusted it was by a fairy who was conversant with the painful circumstances under which she had made her pilgrimage, caused her to hope that the ointment would prove efficacious in removing the disorder under which her child was labouring; but this vague feeling, based as it was upon the mysterious nature of the gift, was accompanied by a perfectly natural fear that, after all, the giver might have been one of those mischievous beings whose delight it was to wreak harm and wrong upon humanity.

When she reached home and told the strange story to her wondering husband, the nervous pair decided that the ointment should not be used unless a further mark of fairy interest in the child's welfare were vouchsafed to them; but when a few days had passed, and the child continued to grow worse, the anxious mother, in the absence of her husband, determined to test the salve upon one of her own eyes. She did so, and after a few minutes of dreadful suspense, finding that evil results did not follow, and saying to herself that surely the fairy could not be desirous of harming her child, she anointed the little girl's eyes. She refrained, however, from making her helpmate acquainted with what she had done, until in the course of a few days the child's eyesight was so nearly restored that it was no longer necessary or possible to keep the matter from him. Great were the rejoicings of the worthy pair over their little one's recovery; but there was not for a very long time any opportunity afforded them of expressing their gratitude.

Some years had passed,—and, as the girl had never had a relapse, the strange gift was almost forgotten,—when one day, in the market-place at Preston, the woman, who was haggling about the price of a load of potatoes, saw before her the identical little fellow in green attire from whom, long before, she had received the box of wonder-working ointment. Although he was busily engaged in a pursuit in which, perhaps, few gentlemen would care to be interrupted, that of stealing corn from an open sack, the thoughtless woman, regardless of etiquette, and yielding to the sudden impulse which prompted her to thank him, stepped forward, and, grasping the fairy's hand, gave utterance to her gratitude.

To her surprise, however, the little fellow seemed very angry with her, and, instead of acknowledging her thanks, hastily asked if she could see him with both eyes, and if she had used the ointment intended for her child. The frightened woman at once said that she saw him with only one eye, and was entering into a long account of the circumstances under which, with maternal instinct, she had tested the value of the gift, when, without more ado, the irritated fairy struck her a violent blow and vanished, and from that time forward the poor woman, instead of being able to see better than her neighbours, was blind of one eye. The daughter, however, often saw the fairies, but, profiting by her mother's painful experience, she was wise enough to refrain from speaking to them either when they gathered by moonlight beneath the trees or in broad daylight broke the Eighth Commandment, utterly unconscious that they were observed by a mortal to whom had been given the wondrous gift of fairy vision.

Satan's Supper

I.

Ye Evil One giveth unto them a stayve.

The 'Old Lad' sat upon his throne,
Beneath a blasted oak,
And fiddled to the mandrake's groan,
The marsh-frog's lonely croak;

II.

Ye corpses dashe their wigges.

Whilst winds they hissed, and shrieked, and moaned
About the branches bare,
And all around the corpses groaned,
And shook their mould'ring hair;

III.

Ye hagges crowde to ye *levee*.

As witches gathered one by one,
And knelt at Satan's feet,
With faces some all worn and wan,
And some with features sweet,

IV.

Ye power of Musicke.

The earth did ope and imps upsprang
Of every shape and shade,
Who 'gan to dance as th' welkin rang
With tunes the 'Old Lad' played;

V.

Ye poetrie of motion.

At which the witches clapped their hands,
And laughed and screamed in glee;
Or jumped about in whirling bands,
And hopped in revelry,

VI.

Ye delicacies of ye season,

Till Satan ceased, when all did rest,
And swarmed unto the meat:
The flesh of infants from the breast,
The toes from dead men's feet,

VII.

Ye ditto,

With sand for salt, and brimstone cates,
With blood for old wine red;
On glittering dish and golden plates
The dainty food was spread.

VIII.

Ye coolinge drinkes.

From heavy cups, with jewels rough,
The witches quenched their thirst;
Yet not before the ruddie stuff
Had been by Satan cursed.

IX.

Ye barde telleth of an outcaste impe.

But one lank fiend of skin and bone,
With hungry-looking eyne,
Gazed at the food with dreary moans,
And many a mournful whine;

X.

Of hys unparalleled wickednesse;

For Satan would not let him feed
Upon the toothsome cheer,
(He had not done all day a deed
To cause a human tear);

XI.

Of hys gamboles and praieres,

And so he hopped from side to side,
To beg a bit of 'toke,'
And, vagrant-like, his plea denied,
He prayed that they might choke

XII.

And of hys revylyngs of goode menne.

Themselves with morsels rich and fat
Or die upon the floor,
Like paupers (grieving much thereat
The guardians of the poor).

XIII.

Ye earlie byrde prepareth for ye 'Diet of Wormes.'

A cock then flapped his wings and crew,
Announcing coming light;
When, seizing on a jar of stew,
The snubbed imp took his flight.

XIV.

Les Adieux.

And at the solemn sound of doom
The witches flew away,
While Satan slunk off through the gloom,
Afraid of break of day;

XV.

Ye fruitlesse remorse of Beelzebubbe.

And in the darkness drear he cried—
His voice a trifle gruff,
'Those omelettes were nicely fried;
I have not had enough!'

XVI.

Ye resulte of ye meetynge uponne ye

A blight fell on the trembling flowers
And on the quivering trees—
No buds there drink the passing showers,
Or leaves wave in the breeze;

XVII.

Agryculture of ye dystricte.

For Satan's presence withered all
The daisies and the grass,
And all things over which like pall
His sulphurous tail did pass.

The Earthenware Goose

Once upon a time, which somewhat vague reference in this instance means long before it was considered a compliment by the fair dames of Lancashire to be termed witches, there lived in the Fylde country village of Singleton a toothless, hooknosed old woman, whose ill fortune it was to be credited with the friendship of the Evil One. Perhaps had the ancient dame been somewhat better looking she might have borne a better character. In those distant days to be poor was considered decidedly discreditable, but to be ugly also was to add insult to injury. The old woman knew only too well that she was poor and that she was plain, for the urchins and hobbledehoys of the locality lost no opportunity of reminding her of the facts, whenever, on frugal mind intent, she emerged from her rude cottage to expend a few pence upon articles of food.

Ugliness and poverty, however, Mag Shelton persisted in considering misfortunes and not crimes, and when anybody to whom she was an eyesore, with gallantry peculiar to the time and place let us hope, wished that she would die and rid the village of her objectionable presence, the old woman took no notice of the polite expression. To die by particular desire was not in Mag's line. What harm could a toothless old woman do, that the world, by which term the half-dazed creature meant the village in which she had spent her life, should evince so much anxiety to be rid of her?—argued Mag. True, if toothless, she had her tongue; but without a visiting circle, and with no benefactors to belie, that valuable weapon in the service of spite might just as well have been in the mouth of an uneducated heathen. Harmless, however, as the old dame thought herself, the villagers held a different opinion, and the children, afraid of disturbing the witch, invariably removed their wooden-soled clogs before they ran past the hut in which Mag lived, while the older folk, if they did not literally take the coverings from their feet as they passed the lonely dwelling, crept by on tiptoe, and glanced furtively at the unsuspecting inhabitant of the cottage, who, by the aid of the fitful firelight, might be seen dozing near the dying embers, and now and again stroking a suspiciously bright-eyed cat, nestled snugly upon her knee.

The old woman's solitary way of life favoured the growth of superstitions regarding her, for the Singletonians were not without their share of that comforting vanity which impresses the provincial mind with a sense of the high importance of its society, parish, and creed; and they could not imagine anyone preferring to keep away from them and to sit alone, without at once believing, as a necessary consequence, that the unappreciative ones must have dealings with Satan.

It soon was found convenient to attribute anything and everything of an unpleasant nature to the denizen of the lonely cottage, 'th' Owd Witch,' as she was termed. Was a cow or a child ailing? Mag had done it! Had the housewife omitted to mark with the sign of the cross the baking of dough left in the mug on the hearth, and the bread had turned out 'heavy,' Mag Shelton had taken advantage of the overworked woman's negligence! Was there but a poor field of wheat? 'Twas the fault of old Mag, swore the farmer. In short, whatever went wrong throughout the entire country-side was judged to be clearly traceable to the spite and malevolence of the toothless old woman and her suspicious-looking cat.

This state of things might, however, have continued without any interruption, until Nature had interposed and released Mag from her attendance upon such a world, had it not begun to be noticed that almost every farmer in the neighbourhood was complaining of the mysterious disappearance of milk, not only from the dairies, but also from the udders of the cows grazing in the pastures. A bucolic genius immediately proclaimed that in this case, too, the culprit must be Mag, for had not she her familiars to feed, and what could be more agreeable to the palate of a parched fiend or perspiring imp, than a beaker of milk fresh from the cow and redolent of meadow-flowers? With such a gaping family to satisfy, what regard could the old lady retain for the Eighth Commandment?

This logic was deemed unanswerable, and a number of the farmers determined to conceal themselves one night about the witch's cottage, in the hope of something confirmatory turning up. It was late when they took their places, and they barely had settled themselves comfortably behind the hedgerow before a noise was heard, and the old woman emerged from the house,—the cat, and, of all things else in the world, a stately goose solemnly paddling behind her.

The men in ambush remained silent until Mag and her attendants had passed out of sight and hearing, when one of them said, 'Keep still, chaps, till hoo comes back. Hoo's gone a milkin', I daat.' The watchers therefore kept perfectly quiet, and in a little while their patience was rewarded; for the old woman reappeared, walking slowly and unattended by her former companions. As she paused to unfasten the cottage door, the men pounced out of their hiding-place, seized her roughly, and at once tore off her cloak. To the surprise of the rude assailants, however, no sign of milk jugs could be observed; and, as they stood aghast, Mag cried, in a shrill and angry voice,

'Will ye never learn to respect grey hair, ye knaves?' 'We'll respect tha' into th' pit yon, mi lady,' immediately responded one of the roughest of the men. 'What hes ta done with th' milk to-neet?'

In vain were the old woman's protestations,—that, driven from the roads and lanes in the daytime by the children and the hobbledehoys who persecuted her, she had of late taken her exercise by night; the judicial mind was made up, and rude hands were outstretched to drag her to the horsepond, when, fortunately for Mag, the appearance of the goose, waddling in a hurried and agitated manner, created a timely diversion in her favour.

'I thowt it quare,' said one of the would-be executioners—'varra quare, that th' goose worn't somewheer abaat, for hoo an' it's as thick as Darby an' Jooan.'

As though conscious that all was not well with its mistress, the ungainly and excited bird, stretching its neck towards the bystanders, and hissing loudly, placed itself by the old woman's side.

'We want no hissin' heear,' said the leader of the band, as he lifted a heavy stick and struck the sibilant fowl a sharp rap on its head.

No sooner had the sound of the blow fallen upon the ears of the assembled rustics than the goose vanished, not a solitary feather being left behind, and in its place there stood a large broken pitcher, from which milk, warm from the cow, was streaming. Here was proof to satisfy even the most credulous, and, as a consequence, in a moment the old woman was floundering in the pond, from which she barely escaped with her life. A few days afterwards, however, upon the interposition of the Vicar, she was permitted to leave the inhospitable village, and away she tramped in search of 'fresh woods and pastures new,' her cat and the revivified goose bearing her company.

She had left the inhospitable place, when the landlord of the Blue Pig discovered that the jug in which the witch-watchers had conveyed their 'allowance' to the place of ambush had not been returned. It was not again seen in its entirety, and the sarcastic host often vowed that it was here and there in the village in the shape of cherished fragments of the broken one into which the watchers declared that they had seen Mag's goose transformed.

The Phantom of the Fell

On a beautiful night late in summer a solitary man, who was returning from some wedding festivities, was rapidly crossing Fair Snape. The moon was at the full, and threw her glamour upon the lovely fell, as a breeze sighed among the tall ferns which waved gently to and fro under the sweet invisible influence, and the only sounds which fell upon the wayfarer's ear were the almost inaudible rustling of the bracken, and the occasional faint bark of a distant watch-dog. Giles Roper, however, was not thinking of the beauty of the night, or of the scenery, but, naturally enough, was congratulating himself upon being ever so much nearer to the stocking of that farm without which he could not hope for the hand of the miller's rosy daughter. Thoughts of a chubby, good-hearted little woman like Liza were calculated to drive out all other and less pleasant ones; but Giles was rapidly approaching a part of the hillside said to be haunted.

Many tales had he heard by the winter's fire of the doings of the nameless appearance, the narrators speaking in hushed voices, and the hearers instinctively drawing closer together on the old settle; and these narratives crowded into his recollection as he left the cheerful moonlight and stepped into the shade of the little clough. Before he had got very far down he was prepared to see or hear anything; but, making allowance for the fear which somehow or other had taken possession of him, he knew that there was something more than fancy in a melancholy wail which broke upon his ears as he reached a bend in the ravine.

There was nothing however in the sad note of lamentation calculated to terrify, save the consciousness that such sweet music could not be that of a mortal.

Instinctively Giles looked in the direction whence the sound had come, and in the dim light he saw the figure of a woman with a pallid face of singular and unearthly beauty, her hair falling behind her like a sheet of gold, and her eyes emitting a strange lustre, which, however, was not sufficiently intense to conceal their beautiful azure hue. The bewildered spectator gazed in rapt worship, for though his limbs still trembled he no longer felt any fear, but rather a wild delirious longing to speak to, and to be addressed by, the beautiful being before him. He was sufficiently near to the appearance to be able to distinguish the features clearly, and when he saw a movement of the lips his heart throbbed violently under the expectation that he was about to receive a mysterious commission.

He was, however, doomed to be disappointed, for the only sound emitted by the phantom was another low melodious cry, even more pathetic and mournful than that by which his attention had first been attracted to the lovely object. At the same time Giles saw that the figure was more distant than before, and that it was slowly gliding away, but beckoning to him, as though anxious that he should follow.

The young man, spell-bound and fascinated by the enchanting eyes, which were beautiful enough to turn the head of one wiser than the raw country lad upon whom they were fixed, followed eagerly, but at the end of the clough, where the moonlight was brilliant, the figure vanished, leaving Giles, not with that feeling of relief said to follow the disappearance of a mysterious visitant, but, on the contrary, anxious to behold the vision again. He therefore turned and retraced his steps to the undulating summit of the fell, where the wind was sighing over the many-flowered heather, but there was nothing to be seen of the blue-eyed phantom, and only for the faint wash of the rustling ferns all would have been silent.

Unwilling to leave the spot, although he was conscious that the task was a fruitless one, he continued to wander from one point to another, and it was not until daybreak that he finally gave up the search and descended the fell. Not caring to allude to his adventure and vain search upon the pike, Giles accounted for his lateness by asserting that he had remained until midnight at the distant farmhouse where the rejoicings had taken place, and had afterwards lost his way on the fells. With this excuse, however, his relatives were quite content, one sarcastic farm-servant drily remarking that after wedding festivities it was wonderful he had been able to find his way home at all.

The extraordinary thoughtfulness which Giles evinced during the day was of too marked a nature to remain unobserved; but the old father attributed it merely to that natural dislike to settled labour which generally follows boisterous relaxation, and the mother thought it was due to a desire to be off again to see the chubby daughter of the miller. The old dame, therefore, was not surprised when her son announced his intention to leave home for a few hours, and she congratulated herself on her foresight and discernment, finishing her soliloquy by saying—'Well, hoo's a bonny wench as he's after; an', what's mooar, hoo's as good as hoo's pratty.'

It was not, however, to the far-off dwelling of the miller that Giles was making his way.

On the contrary, he was leisurely pacing in quite an opposite direction, his back turned to the old mill, and his eyes fixed upon the distant fells, which he did not care to reach until the gloaming had given way to moonlight.

Not that he was afraid of being seen, the road he trod was too lonely for that; but he thought it was unlikely his watchings would be rewarded before the night had properly set in. If the beautiful object was a spirit—and what else could it have been?—it would come at its own time, and who ever heard of spirits appearing before midnight? The young fellow, therefore, waited until the moon rose and bathed the hills in her golden flood, when he at once began to climb the fell, making his way up the ravine in which on the previous night he had heard the mysterious voice.

It was some time from midnight, and he stopped to rest, taking his seat upon a moss-covered stone. Here he waited patiently; but he had begun to fear that his visit was to be a fruitless one, when once more he heard the peculiar mournful wail, and rapidly turning round, he saw that he was not alone. Again the weird eyes, in all their unearthly beauty, were fixed upon him, and the long white arms were extended as though to beckon him to draw nigh.

Instinctively Giles rose in obedience to the pleading attitude of the fair vision; but as he approached the phantom it grew less and less distinct, and at length vanished. As on the previous night, the young fellow wandered about in the hope of again seeing the lovely being, and once more he was obliged to return to the farm unsuccessful.

Possessed by a maddening and irresistible desire to gaze upon the wondrous face which had bewitched him, the approach of nightfall invariably found Giles on his way to the fell, and it can easily be imagined to what unpleasantness in his family circle this course of conduct gave rise.

On the one hand the parents gave the rein to all sorts of vague suspicions as to the cause of the night rambles; and the lad's disinclination to give any explanations did not help the old people to think more kindly of him. The father of the girl whom he had asked in marriage also did not fail to expostulate with him, in the idea that he had fallen into evil ways, and that his pilgrimages were to a distant town; while the girl herself, loving him as she did with all the vigour of her simple and earnest nature, and uninfluenced by any foolish feeling of false shame, came to his parents' house in the hope of obtaining a promise of better things.

Her pleadings and her womanly threats, however, were unavailing, the whilom lover in a shamefaced manner refusing to make any promise of different behaviour. The interview was a painful one; for the girl, feeling certain that her father's interpretation was correct, used all her powers to induce Giles to abandon his evil courses; but at length, finding that her prayers were ineffectual, she bitterly reproached him with his want of honesty.

'It's no evil as I'm after, lass! Don't think that on mi,' said the young man, in an appealing tone; but the girl was not to be convinced by mere assertion.

'It's no good as teks tha away o'er t' pike neet after neet,' said she, with a sudden access of grief, 'it'ull come by tha in some way or another, Giles.' And in tears she turned away from him.

'Whisht, lass, whisht! If tha nobbut knew, O tha'd pity i'stid o' blaming mi.'

The girl heeded not these words, but kept on her way. When she got to a turn in the road, however, she looked back mournfully, as though in doubt whether to return and cast herself upon his breast, and bid him trust in her; but pride overcame her, and she resisted the impulse.

That night, as two of the miller's men were poaching, they were startled by the unexpected sound of a human voice, and hastily hiding themselves beneath the tall ferns, they saw Giles emerge from the clough and run towards the place where they were concealed. He seemed to be half mad with excitement, and as he ran he was crying aloud some words they could not catch. When he drew nearer, however, they were able to hear more distinctly, and to their surprise they found that he was appealing to an invisible being to appear to him.

For some time they remained in their place of concealment, Giles hovering about the spot; but when the young fellow ran to a distance, they emerged from their hiding-place and rapidly made their way to the mill. For obvious reasons, however, they agreed to keep silence as to what they had seen and heard.

The day after this episode Giles was in a fever and delirious, raving continually about the bonny face and 'breet een' of the being he had seen in the ravine. His afflicted parents found in the wild utterances sad confirmation of their worst fears, and, half broken-hearted, they hovered sorrowfully about his bed. For weeks he battled with the disorder, and at nightfall frequently endeavoured to leave the house, and vainly struggled with the friends who prevented him, to whom he frantically cried that she of the blue eyes was calling him.

A cloud fell over the hitherto happy household. Night and day the old people watched over their sick lad, each of them feeling that the task would have been a comparatively easy one had not the patient's delirious ravings revealed to them so terrible a background to the round of their primitive and innocent daily life. Not that they loved their child any less because of the revelations he had unconsciously made to them, but they brooded and fretted over his supposed wickedness, and bowed their heads in grief and shame as they unwillingly heard his impassioned cries.

By-and-by the story of these ravings got noised about, and the miller's daughter, who hitherto had been suffering bravely, broke down altogether when she knew that she was an object of pity to the gossips. It fortunately happened, however, that the miller's men who had seen Giles at the pike got into conversation with their master about the matter, and it struck one of them that the woman about whom Giles was supposed to be raving, and of whom tales of all sorts were being circulated, was a feeorin of some kind that the young fellow had seen on the lonely fell. No sooner was this idea arrived at than off they started to see the distressed parents, the miller's daughter hastening with them. They found no difficulty in gaining credence for their narrative, and with a burst of thankfulness the old people felt that the gulf which had yawned between them and their eldest born was for ever closed; while, as for the girl, her transports of joy were almost painful in their intensity. So great a weight was lifted from all hearts that the illness of the patient was for the time almost forgotten. Giles, however, still remained in a very critical condition, but he soon had an additional nurse, who, despite the watchings and the toil of which she relieved the old people, was rapidly becoming more and more like the ruddy-faced damsel to whom the young fellow had plighted his troth, for she could listen to and disregard the ravings of her lover and look forward to the time when happiness should again smile upon them.

A few weeks passed. The violence of the disorder abated, and the patient recovered so far as to be able to bear removal to a large chair by the kitchen fire. As he sat quietly dreaming the short autumn days away, without any allusions to the beauty about whom he had so constantly raved during his delirium, the old people and the miller's daughter began to congratulate themselves that the dream-madness had passed away with the worst phase of the illness.

The girl, however, although she did not utter any complaint, suffered deeply from the coolness with which Giles treated her. Not that he was ungrateful, for, on the contrary, it was impossible to do anything for him, however slight the service might be, without a thankful acknowledgment; but there was a visible constraint in his manner which could not escape the keen sight of love. Fearing to distress him by any remonstrances, the patient girl refrained from referring to the past or showing that she was observant of any change in his behaviour towards her, but she brooded over her grief when she was alone. The young fellow knew that the poor girl was suffering, but for the life of him he could not assume that which did not feel. Much as he had loved her before the night of his adventure on the pike, from the moment when he had first seen the face of the mysterious being his affection for her had faded away, consumed by the intense longing which filled his soul night and day whenever he thought of the eyes illumined by a fire that was not human, and of the features and hair so exquisitely beautiful in the faint moonlight. Calm and

114

quiet as he looked, seated propped with cushions in the old chair by the fire, he was inwardly fretting against the weakness that kept him from the fells, and his longing soul came into his eyes as he gazed through the little diamond-paned window, and saw the pike, in all the beauty of many-tinted autumn, kissed by the setting sun as the blushing day sank into the swarthy arms of night.

Slowly winter came, bringing snow and storm, and as though influenced by a feeling that even Nature had interposed her barriers between him and the lovely being, one afternoon, as the mists crept slowly over the white landscape, and hid in their shimmering folds the distant fells where he had first seen the sweet face so seldom absent from his feverish dreams, he could not resist the desire which seized him to visit once more the haunted ravine. The various members of the little household were away from the house engaged in their labours about the farm, and taking advantage of this, Giles fled from the dwelling, and made his way through the dim light to the hills. It was not long, however, before his absence was discovered, but some time elapsed before the men-folk could be gathered, and the shades of night had fallen before the anxious pursuers reached the foot of the pike.

The thick mist had enveloped everything, and as the lanterns, choked as they were by the damp, threw but a fitful light, it was with the utmost difficulty that the men found the footmarks of the wanderer in the snow up the fell side. The searchers were led by the father of Giles, who spoke not, but glanced at the track as though in dread of discovering that which he had come to find. Suddenly the old man gave a startled cry, for he had followed the marks to the edge of a little cliff, over which he had almost fallen in his eagerness. It was forthwith determined to follow the ravine to its commencement, and although nothing was said by any of the party, each man felt certain that the missing young fellow would be found at the bottom. It did not take long to reach the entrance, and with careful steps the old man led the way over the boulders. He had not gone far before the light from his lantern fell upon the upturned face of his son, whose body lay across the course of a little frozen stream. The features were set in the sleep of death, for Giles had fallen from the level above, the creeping mists having obscured the gorge where he first saw the lovely phantom, in search of which he had met an untimely end.

Allhallow's Night

To many a beautiful landscape the majestic Pendle adds a nameless charm, and the traveller who gazes upon it from any of the points whence a view of the whalelike mass is to be obtained, would hardly dream that the moss and fern-covered hill, smiling through the dim haze, once was the headquarters of witchcraft and devilry. Readers of the quaint and sad trials of the witchmania period, and of Harrison Ainsworth's celebrated novel based thereon, will, however, remember what dread scenes were said to have transpired in the dim light of its cloughs and upon its wild sides, when Chattox, Mouldheels, and the other poor wretches whose 'devilish practices and hellish means,' as they were termed in the old indictments, made the neighbourhood of the mountain so unsafe a locality.

In a lonely little house some distance from the foot of Pendle, there dwelt a farmer and his family, together with a labourer whom he employed. Entirely illiterate, and living in a wild and weird district, with but few houses nearer than a mile away, the household believed firmly in all the dreadful boggart, witch, and feeorin stories current in the district. For a long time, however, the farmer had not any personal experience of the power of either witch or boggart; but at length his turn came. After a tempestuous night, when the windows and doors rattled in their frames, and the wind, dashing the big rain drops against the little diamond-shaped panes, moaned and shrieked round the lonely dwelling, three of the beasts were found dead in the shippon. A few days afterwards two of the children sickened, and when 'th' edge o' dark' was creeping up the hill-side one of them died. As though this trouble was not enough, the crops were blighted. With reluctance the farmer saw in these things proof that he had in some unknown manner incurred the displeasure of the invisible powers, and that the horse-shoe over his door, the branches of ash over the entrance to the shippon, and the hag stones hung up at the head of his own and of the children's bed, had lost their power of protection.

The family council, at which the unprotected condition of the house was discussed, was of the saddest kind, for even the rough labourer missed the prattle of the little one whose untimely end had cast a shadow over the dwelling, and he thoroughly sympathised with his master in his losses; while, as for the farmer and his wife, dread of what the future might have in store for them mingled with their sorrow, and added to the heaviness of their hearts.

'Isaac, yo' may as weel tek' th' wiggin an' th' horse shoes deawn, for onny use they seem to be on. We'en nowt to keep th' feorin' off fra' us, an' I deawt we'es come off bud badly till November,' said the farmer, as he knocked the ashes from his pipe.

'An' why nobbut till November, Ralph,' asked the wife in a terrified voice, as she gazed anxiously towards the little window through which Pendle could be dimly seen looming against the evening sky.

'Because on O'Hallow neet, mi lass, I meean to leet th' witches on Pendle.'

'Heaven save us!' cried the woman. 'Tha'll be lost as sewer as th' whorld.'

There was a short silence, and then old Isaac spoke—

'If th' mestur goes, Isik guz too. Wis be company, at onny rate.'

The farmer gratefully accepted this offer of fellowship, and the appeals of his wife, who implored him to abandon the notion, were of no avail. Others had lighted the witches, and thereby secured a twelvemonth's immunity from harm, and why should not he go and do likewise? Ruin was staring him in the face if things did not improve, thought he, and his determination to 'leet' his unseen enemies grew stronger and stronger.

At length the last day of October came, bringing with it huge clouds and a misty rain, which quite obscured the weird hill; but at nightfall the wind rose, the rain ceased, the stars began to appear, and the huge outline of Pendle became visible.

When the day's work was over, the farmer and Isaac sat in the kitchen, waiting for the hour at which they were to start for the haunted mountain, and the dread and lonesome building where the witches from all parts gathered in mysterious and infernal conclave. Neither of the men looked forward to the excursion with pleasurable feelings, for, as the emotion caused by the losses had somewhat subsided, terror of the beings who were supposed to assemble in the Malkin Tower resumed its sway; but soon after the old clock had chimed ten they rose from the settle and began their preparations for the lighting. Each man grasped a branch of mountain ash, to which several sprigs of bay were tied as a double protection against thunder and lightning, and any stray fiends that might happen to be lurking about, and each carried in the other hand an unlighted candle.

As they passed from the house the tearful goodwife cried a blessing upon them, and a massive old bulldog crept from a corner of the yard and took its place at their heels.

The three stepped along bravely, and before long they had crossed the brook and reached the foot of Pendle. Rapidly making their way to a well-known ravine they paused to light the candles. This operation, performed by means of a flint and steel and a box of tinder, occupied some time; and while they were so engaged clouds obscured the moon, a few heavy drops of rain fell, the wind ceased to whisper, and an ominous silence reigned, and the dog, as though terrified, crept closer to its master and uttered a low whine.

'We's hev' a storm, I daat, Isik,' said the farmer.

'Ise think mysen weel off an' win nowt else bud a storm,' drily replied the old man, as, lighted candle in hand, he began to climb the hill-side, his master and the dog following closely behind.

When they had almost reached the top of the ravine a flash of lightning suddenly pierced the darkness, and a peal of thunder seemed to shake the earth beneath them; while a weird and unearthly shriek of laughter rang in their ears as a black figure flew slowly past them, almost brushing against their faces in its flight. The dog immediately turned and fled, howling terribly as it ran down the hill-side; but the men went on, each one carefully shading his light with the hand in which the branch of ash was grasped. The road gradually became rougher, and occasionally Isaac stumbled over a stone, and almost fell, the farmer frantically shouting to him to be careful of his candle, but without any serious mishap the pair managed to get within sight of the tower.

Evidently some infernal revelry was going on, for light streamed from the window-openings, and above the crash of the thunder came shrieks of discordant laughter. Every now and again a dark figure floated over their heads and whirled in at one of the windows, and the noise became louder, by the addition of another shrill voice.

'It mon be drawin' nee midneet,' said the farmer. 'If we con but pass th' hour wis be reet for a twelvemonth. Let's mek for whoam neaw.'

Both men readily turned their backs to the building, but no sooner had they done so than a Satanic face, with gleaming eyes, was visible for a moment, and instantaneously both lights were extinguished.

'God bless us!' immediately cried both men.

Almost before the words had left their lips the tower was plunged in total darkness, the shrieks of unholy laughter were suddenly stilled, and sounds were heard as of the rapid flight of the hags and their familiars, for the ejaculations had broken up the gathering.

Terrified beyond measure at the extinction of their lights, but still clinging tenaciously to the branches, which apparently had proved so ineffectual to preserve them against the power of the witches, the men hurried away. They had not proceeded far in the direction in which they supposed the farm lay, when, with a cry, the farmer, who was a little in advance of his aged companion, fell and vanished. He had slipped down the cleft, on the brink of which Isaac stood, tremblingly endeavouring to pierce the darkness below.

Not a sound came up to tell the old man that his master had escaped with his life; and, as no response came to his shouts, at length he turned away, feeling sure that he was masterless, and hoping to be able to reach the farm, and obtain assistance. After wandering about for some time, however, half-blinded by the lightning, and terrified beyond measure at the result of their mutual boldness, Isaac crept under a large stone, to wait for the dawn. Influenced by the cold and by fatigue, the old man fell asleep; but no sooner had the first faint rays of coming day kissed the hill-summit, than he was aroused by the old bulldog licking his face, and as he gazed around in sleepy astonishment some men appeared. The farmer's wife, terrified by the arrival of the howling dog, and the non-arrival of the 'leeters,' had made her way to a distant farm-house and alarmed the inmates, and a party of sturdy fellows had started off to find the missing men. Isaac's story was soon told; and when the searchers reached the gorge the farmer was found nursing a broken leg.

Great were the rejoicings of the goodwife when the cavalcade reached the farm, for, bad as matters were, she had expected even a worse ending; and afterwards, when unwonted prosperity had blessed the household, she used to say, drily, 'Yo' met ha' kept th' candles in to leet yo' whoam, for it mon ha' bin after midneet when *he* blew 'em aat,' a joke which invariably caused the farmer and old Isaac to smile grimly.

The Christmas Eve Vigil

Many years have passed since the living of Walton-le-Dale was held by a gentleman of singularly-reserved and studious habits, who, from noon till night, pored over dusty black-letter folios. Although he was by no means forgetful of the few duties which pertained to his sacred office, and never failed to attend to the wants of those of his parishioners who were in trouble and had need of kind words of sympathy and advice, or even of assistance of a more substantial nature, the length of time he devoted to his mysterious-looking volumes, and a habit he had of talking to himself, as, late at night, with head bent down, he passed along the village street, and vanished into the darkness of a lonely lane, gave rise to cruel rumours that he was a professor of the black art; and it was even whispered that his night walks were pilgrimages to unholy scenes of Satanic revelry. These suspicions deepened almost into certainty when the old people who had charge of his house informed the gossips that the contents of a large package, since the arrival of which the women in the village had been unable to sleep for curiosity, were strange-looking bottles, of a weird shape, with awful signs and figures upon them; and that, during the evening, after the carrier had brought them, noises were heard in the clergyman's room, and the house was filled with sulphurous smoke. Passing from one gossip to another, the story did not fail to receive additions as usual, until when it reached the last house in the straggling village the narrator told how the student had raised the Evil One, who, after filling the house with brimstone, vanished in a ball of fire, not, however, without first having imprinted the mark of his claws upon the study table.

Had the unconscious clergyman lived more in the everyday world around him, and less in that of black-letter books, he would not have failed to perceive the averted looks with which his parishioners acknowledged his greetings, or, what would have pained him even more deeply, the frightened manner in which the children either fled at his approach, if they were playing in the lanes, or crept close to their parents when he entered the dwellings of the cottagers. Ignorant alike of the absurd rumours, and unobservant of the change which had come over his flock, or at least acting as though unaware of them, the clergyman continued to perform the duties of his sacred office, and to fly from them to his beloved volumes and experiments, growing more and more reserved in his habits, and visibly paling under his close application.

After matters had gone on in this way for some time, the villagers were surprised to see a friendship spring up and ripen between their pastor and an old resident in the village, of almost equally strange habits. There was, however, in reality but little to wonder at in this, for the similarity between the pursuits and tastes of the two students was sufficiently great to bridge over the gulf of widely-different social positions.

Abraham, or 'Owd Abrum,' as he was generally named, was a herb doctor, whose knowledge of out-of-the-way plants which possessed mysterious medicinal virtues, and of still more wonderful charms and spells, was the theme of conversation by every farmhouse fireside for miles round. At that day, and in that locality, the possession of a few books sufficed to make a man a wonder to his neighbours; and Abraham had a little shelf full of volumes upon his favourite subjects of botany and astrology.

The old man lived by himself in a little cottage, some distance along a lane leading from the village across the meadows; and, despite the absence of female supervision, the place always was as clean and bright as a new pin. Had he needed any assistance in his household duties, Abraham would not have asked in vain for it, for he was feared as well as respected. If he was able to charm away evil and sickness, could he not also bring sickness and evil? So reasoned the simple villagers; and those who were not, even unconsciously, influenced by the guileless everyday life of the old man, were impressed by the idea that he had the power to cast trouble upon them if they failed to maintain an outward show of reverence.

However early the villagers might be astir, as they passed along the lanes on their way to their labour in the fields, they were certain to find 'Owd Abrum' searching by the hedgerows or in the plantations for herbs, to be gathered with the dew upon them; and at night the belated cottager, returning from a distant farm, was equally certain of finding Abraham gazing at the heavens, 'finding things aat abaat fowk,' as the superstitious country people said and believed.

Addicted to such nocturnal studies, it was not likely that the old herb doctor and the pale student would remain unknown to each other. The acquaintance however, owing to the reserved habits of both, began in a somewhat singular manner. Returning from a long and late walk about midnight, the minister was still some distance from his abode, when he heard a clear voice say: 'Now is the time, if I can find any: Jupiter is angular, the moon's applied to him, and his aspect is good.'

The night was somewhat cloudy—the stars being visible only at intervals—and it was not until the clergyman had advanced a little way that he was able to perceive the person who had spoken. He saw that it was the old herbalist, and immediately accosted him. An animated conversation followed, Abraham expatiating on the virtues of the plants he had been gathering under the dominion of their respective planets, and astonishing the pale student by the extent of his information. In his turn, the old man was delighted to find in the clergyman a fellow-enthusiast in the forbidden ways of science; and as the student was no less charmed to discover in the 'yarb doctor' a scholar who could sympathise with him and understand his yearnings after the invisible, late as was the hour, the pair adjourned to Abraham's cottage. The visitor did not emerge until the labourers were going to their toil, the time having been spent in conversation upon the powers exercised by the planets upon plants and men, the old man growing eloquent as to the wonderful virtue of the Bay Tree, which, he said, could resist all the evil Saturn could do to the human body, and in the neighbourhood of which neither wizard nor devil, thunder or lightning, could hurt man; of Moonwort, with the leaves of which locks might be opened, and the shoes be removed from horses' feet; of Celandine, with which, if a young swallow loseth an eye, the parent birds will renew it; of Hound's Tongue, a leaf of which laid under the foot will save the bearer from the attacks of dogs; of Bugloss, the leaf of which maketh man poison-proof; of Sweet Basil, from which (quoting Miraldus) venomous beasts spring—the man who smelleth it having a scorpion bred in his brain; and of a score of other herbs under the dominion of the Moon and Cancer, and of the cures wrought by them through antipathy to Saturn.

From that time the pair became intimate friends, the clergyman yielding, with all the ardour of youth, to the attraction which drew him towards the learned old man; and Abraham gradually growing to love the pale-faced student, whose thirst after knowledge was as intense as his own. Seldom a day passed on which one of them might not have been observed on his way to the abode of the other; and often at night the pair walked together, their earnest voices disturbing the slumbering echoes, as at unholy hours they passed up the hill, and through the old churchyard, with its moss-covered stones and its rank vegetation.

Upon one of these occasions they had talked about supernatural appearances; and as they were coming through the somewhat neglected God's Acre, the clergyman said he had read, in an old volume, that to anyone who dared, after the performance of certain ghastly ceremonies, wait in the church porch on Christmas-eve, the features of those who were to die during the following year would be revealed, and that he intended upon the night before the coming festival to try the spell. The old man at once expressed a wish to take part in the trial, and before the two parted it was agreed that both should go through the preliminary charms, and keep the vigil.

In due time the winter came, with its sweet anodyne of snow, and as Christmas approached everything was got in readiness.

Soon after sunset on Christmas-eve the old herb doctor wended his way to the dwelling of his friend, taking with him St. John's Wort, Mountain Ash, Bay leaves, and Holly. The enthusiasts passed the evening in conversation upon the mysterious qualities of graveyard plants; but shortly after the clock struck eleven they arose, and began to prepare for the vigil, by taking precautions against the inclemency of the weather, for the night was very cold, large flakes of snow falling silently and thickly upon the frozen ground.

When both were ready the old man stepped to the door to see that the road was clear, for, in order to go through the form of incantation, a small fire was requisite; and as they were about to convey it in a can, they were anxious that the strange proceeding should not be noticed by the villagers. Late as it was, however, lights shone here and there in the windows, and even from the doorways, for, although it was near midnight, many of the cottage doors were wide open, it being believed that if, on Christmas-eve, the way was thus left clear, and a member of the family read the Gospel according to St. Luke, the saint himself would pass through the house.

As the two men, after carefully closing the door behind them, stepped into the road, a distant singer trolled forth a seasonable old hymn. This was the only noise, however, the village street being deserted. They reached the churchyard without having been observed, and at once made their way round the sacred building, so as not to be exposed to the view of any chance reveller returning to his home. It was well that they did so, for they had hardly deposited the can of burning charcoal upon a tombstone ere sounds of footsteps, somewhat muffled by the snow, were heard, and several men passed through the wicket. They were, however, only the ringers, on their way to the belfry, and in a few minutes they had entered the building, and all was still again for a few moments, when, upon the ears of the somewhat nervous men there fell the voices of choristers singing under the window of a neighbouring house the old Lancashire carol—

'As I sat anonder yon green tree,
Yon green tree, yon green tree—

As I sat anonder yon green tree
A Christmas day in the morning.'

The words could be heard distinctly, and almost unconsciously the two men stood to listen; but directly the voices ceased the student asked if they had not better begin, as the time was passing rapidly.

'Ay,' replied Abraham, 'we han it to do, an' we'd better ger it ower.'

Without any more words they entered the porch, and at once made a circle around them with leaves of Vervain, Bay, and Holly. The old man gave to his companion a branch of Wiggintree, and firmly held another little bough, as with his disengaged hand he scattered a powder upon the embers. A faint odour floated around them, as they chanted a singular Latin prayer; and no sooner was the last word uttered than a strain of sweet sad music, too inexpressibly soft and mournful to be of earth, was heard. Every moment it seemed to be dying away in a delicious cadence, but again and again was the weird melody taken up by the invisible singers, as the listeners sank to their knees spell-bound. An icy breath of wind hissed round the porch, however, and called the entranced men to their senses, and suddenly the student grasped the arm of his aged companion, and cried, in a terrified voice—

'Abraham, the spell works. Behold!'

The old man gazed in the direction pointed out, and, to his inexpressible horror, saw a procession wending its way towards the porch. It consisted of a stream of figures wrapped up in grave-clothes, gleaming white in the dim light. With solemn and noiseless steps the ghastly objects approached the circle in which stood the venturesome men, and, as they drew nearer, the faces of the first two could be seen distinctly, for the blazing powder cast a lurid glow upon them, and made them even more ghastly.

Both spectators had almost unconsciously recognised the features of several of the villagers, when they were aroused from their lethargy of terror by the appearance of one face, which seemed to linger longer than its predecessors had done. Abraham at once saw that the likeness was that of the man by his side, and the clergyman sank to the ground in a swoon.

For some time the old man was too much affected by the lingering face to think of restoring the unconscious man at his feet; but at length the clashing of the bells over his head, as they rang forth a Christmas greeting, called him to himself, and he bent over the prostrate form of his friend. The minister soon recovered, but as he was too weak to walk, the old man ran to the belfry to beg the ringers to come to his assistance. When these men came round to the porch the fire was still burning, the flickering flames of various colours casting dancing shadows upon the walls.

'Abraham,' said one of the ringers, 'there's bin some wizzard wark goin' on here, an' yo' sin what yo'n getten by it.'

'Han yo' bin awsin to raise th' devul, an' Kesmus-eve an' o'?' asked another, in a low and terrified voice.

With a satirical smile, Abraham answered the last speaker: 'It dusn't need o' this mak' o' things to raise th' devul, lad. He's nare so far fra' thuse as wants him.'

Bearing the clergyman in their arms, the men walked through the village, but they did not separate without having, in return for the confidence Abraham reposed in them by confiding to them the secret of the vigil, promised strict secrecy as to what they had witnessed.

Abraham's companion soon recovered from the shock, but not before the story of the night-watch had gone the round of the village. Many were the appeals made to the old herbalist to reveal his strangely-acquired knowledge, but Abraham remained sternly obdurate, remarking to each of his questioners—

'Yo'll know soon enough, mebbi.'

The clergyman, however, was in a more awkward position, and his parishioners soon made him aware how unwise he had been in giving way to the desire to pry into futurity; for, when any of them were ill and he expressed a kindly wish for their recovery, it was by no means unusual for the sick person to reply—

'Yo could tell me heaw it will end iv yo' loiked.'

This oftentimes being followed by a petition from the assembled relatives—

'Will yo tell us if he wir one o' th' processioners?'

Ultimately Abraham's companion went away, in the hope of returning when the memory of the watch should have become less keen, but, before a few months had passed away, news came of his death, after a violent attack of fever caught during a visit to a wretched hovel in the fishing village where he was staying. By the next December, all the people whose features the old herbalist had recognised during the procession had been carried to the churchyard; but, although several men offered to accompany Abraham to the porch on the forthcoming Christmas-eve, he dared not again go through the spells and undergo the terrors of a church-porch vigil.

The Crier of Claife

Upon a wild winter night, some centuries ago, the old man who plied the ferry-boat on Windermere, and who lived in a lonely cottage on the Lancashire side of the Lake, was awakened from his sleep by an exceedingly shrill and terrible shriek, which seemed to come from the opposite shore. The wind was whistling and moaning round the house, and for a little while the ferryman and his family fancied that the cry by which they had been disturbed was nothing more than one of the mournful voices of the storm; but soon again came another shriek, even more awe-inspiring than the former one, and this was followed by smothered shouts and groans of a most unearthly nature.

Against the wishes of his terrified relatives, who clung to him, and besought him to remain indoors, the old fellow bravely determined to cross the water, and heeding not the prayers of his wife and daughter, he unfastened his boat, and rowed away. The two women, clasped in each other's arms, trembling with fear, stood at the little door, and endeavoured to make out the form of their protector; but the darkness was too deep for them to see anything upon the lake. At intervals, however, the terrible cry rang out through the gloom, and shrieks and moans were heard loud above the mysterious noises of the night.

In a state of dreadful suspense and terror the women stood for some time, but at length they saw the boat suddenly emerge from the darkness, and shoot into the little cove. To their great surprise, however, the ferryman, who could be seen sitting alone, made no effort to land, and make his way to the cottage; so, fearing that something dreadful had happened to him, and, impelled by love, they rushed to the side of the lake. They found the old man speechless, his face as white and blanched as the snow upon the Nab, and his whole body trembling under the influence of terror, and they immediately led him to the cottage, but though appealed to, to say what terrible object he had seen, he made no other response than an occasional subdued moan. For several days he remained in that state, deaf to their piteous entreaties, and staring at them with wild-looking eyes; but at length the end came, and, during the gloaming of a beautiful day, he died, without having revealed to those around him what he had seen when, in answer to the midnight cry, he had rowed the ferry-boat across the storm-ruffled lake.

After the funeral had taken place the women left the house, its associations being too painful to permit of their stay, and went to live at Hawkshead, whence two sturdy men, with their respective families, removed to the ferry. The day following that of the arrival of the new-comers was rough and wild, and, soon after darkness had hidden everything in its sable folds, across the lake came the fearful cry, followed by a faint shout for a boat, and screams and moans. The men, hardy as they were, and often as they had laughed at the story told by the widow of the dead man, no sooner heard the first shriek ring through the cottage than they were smitten with terror. Profiting, however, by the experience of their predecessor, and influenced by fear, they did not make any attempt to cross the lake, and the cries continued until some time after midnight.

Afterwards, whenever the day closed gloomily, and ushered in a stormy night, and the wind lashed the water of the lake into fury, the terrible noises were heard with startling distinctness, until at length the dwellers in the cottage became so accustomed to the noises as not to be disturbed by them, or, if disturbed, to fall asleep again after an ejaculation of 't' crier!' Pedlars and others who had to cross the lake, however, were not so hardened, and after a time the ferry-boat was almost disused, for the superstitious people did not dare to cross the haunted water, save in the broad daylight of summer.

It therefore struck the two individuals who were most concerned in the maintenance of the ferry that if they intended to live they must do something to rid the place of its bad name, and of the unseen being who had driven away all their patrons. In their extremity they asked each other who should help them, if not the holy monks, who had come over the sea to the abbey in the Valley of Deadly Night Shade; and one of the ferrymen at once set out for Furness. No sooner had he set eyes upon the stately pile erected by the Savignian and his companions than his heart felt lighter, for he had a simple faith in the marvellous power of the white-robed men, whose voices were seldom if ever heard, save when lifted in worship during one of their seven daily services.

Knocking at the massive door, he was received by a ruddy-looking servitor, who ushered him into the presence of the abbot. The ferryman soon told his story, and begged that a monk might return with him to lay the troubled spirit, and after hearing the particulars of the visitation, the abbot granted the request, making a proviso, however, that the abbey coffers should not be forgotten when the lake was freed from the fiend.

No sooner had the visitor finished the meal set before him by the hospitable monks than, in company with one of the holy men, he set out homeward. As, by a rule of his order, the monk was not permitted to converse, the journey was not an enlivening one, and the ferryman was heartily glad when they reached his cottage.

The first night passed without any alarm, the monk and his hosts spending the dreary hours in watching and waiting. The following day, however, was as stormy as the worst enemy of the ferry could have wished, and, when night fell, all the dwellers in the cottage, as well as the silent monk, gathered together again to wait for the cries, but some hours passed without any other sounds having been heard than those caused by the restless wind, as it swept over the lake and among the trees. The Cistercian was beginning to imagine himself the victim of an irreverent practical joke, and that the stories of the spectral crier which had reached the distant abbey long before the ferryman's visit were a pack of falsehoods, when about midnight, he suddenly jumped from the chair upon which he was dozing by the wood fire, hastily made the sign of the cross, and hurriedly commended himself to the protection of his patron saint, for sharp and clear came the dread cry, followed rapidly by a number of shrieks and groans and a smothered appeal for a boat.

In an instant one of the men, with courage doubtless inspired by the presence of the holy man, shouldered the oars and opened the door, and the monk at once stepped into the open air and hurried to the lake, the men following at a respectful distance. The white-robed father was the first to get into the boat, and the ferrymen hoped that he intended to go alone, but he called upon them to propel the boat to the middle of the lake, and much as they disliked the task, as it was on their behalf that the monk was about to combat the evil spirit, they could not well refuse to accompany him.

When they were about half-way across the lake the wind suddenly lulled, and once more they heard the awful scream, and this time it sounded as though the crier was quite close to them. The occupants of the boat were terribly frightened, and one of them, after suddenly shrieking 'he's here,' fainted, and lay still at the bottom of the boat, while the monk and the other man stared straight before them, as though petrified.

There was a fourth person present, a grim and ghastly figure, with the trappings of this life still dangling about its withered and shrunken limbs, and a gaping wound in its pallid throat. For a few minutes there was a dead silence, but at last it was broken by the monk, who rapidly muttered a prayer for protection against evil spirits, and then took a bottle from a pocket of his robe, and sprinkled a few drops of holy water upon himself and the ferryman, who remained in the same statuesque attitude, and upon the unconscious occupant of the bottom of the boat. After this ceremony, he opened a little book, and, in a sonorous voice, intoned the form for the exorcism of a wandering soul, concluding with *Vade ad Gehennam!* when to the infinite relief of the ferryman, and probably of the monk also, the ghastly figure forthwith vanished.

The Cistercian asked to be immediately taken to the shore, and when he neared the house, the little book was again brought into requisition, and the spirit's visits, should it ever again put in an appearance, limited to an old and disused quarry, a distance from the cottage.

From that time to this, the wild, lonely place has indeed been desolate and deserted, the boldest people of the district not having sufficient courage to venture near it at nightfall, and the more timid ones shunning the locality even at noonday. These folks aver that even yet, despite the prayers and exorcisms of the white-robed Cistercian from Furness, whenever a storm descends upon the lake, the Crier escapes from his temporary prison house, and revisits the scene of his first and second appearance to men, and that on such nights, loud above the echoed rumble of the thunder, and the lonely sough of the wind, the benighted wayfarer still hears the wild shrieks and the muffled cry for a boat.

The Demon of the Oak

Once a fortress and a mansion, but now, unfortunately, little more than a noble ruin, Hoghton Tower stands on one of the most commanding sites in Lancashire. From the fine old entrance-gate a beautiful expanse of highly-cultivated land slopes down and stretches away to the distant sea, glimmering like a strip of molten silver; and on either hand there are beautiful woods, in the old times 'so full of tymber that a man passing through could scarce have seen the sun shine in the middle of the day.' At the foot of these wooded heights a little river ripples through a wild ravine, and meanders through the rich meadows to the proud Ribble. From the building itself, however, the glory has departed. Over the noble gateway, with its embattled towers, and in one of the fast-decaying wainscots, the old family arms, with the motto, *Mal Gre le Tort*, still remain; but these things, and a few mouldering portraits, are all that are left there to tell of the stately women who, from the time of Elizabeth down to comparatively modern days, pensively watched the setting sun gild the waters of the far-off Irish Sea, and dreamed of lovers away in the wars—trifling things to be the only unwritten records of the noble men who buckled on their weapons, and climbed into the turrets to gaze over the road along which would come the expected besieging parties. Gone are the gallants and their ladies, the roystering Cavalier and the patient but none the less brave Puritan, for, as Isaac Ambrose has recorded, during the troublous times of the Restoration, the place, with its grand banqueting chamber, its fine old staircases, and quaint little windows, was 'a colledge for religion.' The old Tower resounds no more with the gay song of the one or the solemn hymn of the other,

'Men may come, and men may go,'

and an old tradition outlives them all.

To this once charming mansion there came, long ago, a young man, named Edgar Astley. His sable garments told that he mourned the loss of a relative or friend; and he had not been long at the Tower before it began to be whispered in the servants'-hall that 'the trappings and the suits of woe' were worn in memory of a girl who had been false to him, and who had died soon after her marriage to his rival. This story in itself was sufficient to throw a halo of romance around the young visitor; but when it was rumoured that domestics, who had been returning to the Tower late at night, had seen strange-coloured lights burning in Edgar's room, and that, even at daybreak, the early risers had seen the lights still unextinguished, and the shadow of the watcher pass across the curtains, an element of fear mingled with the feelings with which he was regarded.

There was much in the visitor calculated to deepen the impressions by which the superstitious domestics were influenced, for, surrounded by an atmosphere of gloom, out of which he seemed to start when any of them addressed him, and appearing studiously to shun all the society which it was possible for him to avoid, he spent most of his time alone, seated beneath the spreading branches of the giant oak tree at the end of the garden, reading black-letter volumes, and plunged in meditation. Not that he was in any way rude to his hosts; on the contrary, he was almost chivalrous in his attention to the younger members of the family and to the ladies of the house, who, in their turn, regarded him with affectionate pity, and did their utmost to wean him from his lonely pursuits. Yet, although he would willingly accompany them through the woods, or to the distant town, the approach of the gloaming invariably found him in his usual place beneath the shadow of the gnarled old boughs, either poring over his favourite books, or, with eyes fixed upon vacancy, lost in a reverie.

Time would, the kind people thought, bring balm to his wounds, and in the meanwhile they were glad to have their grief-stricken friend with them; and fully appreciating their sympathy, Edgar came and went about the place and grounds just as the whim of the moment took him. This absence of curiosity on the part of the members of the family was, however, amply compensated for by the open wonder with which many of the domestics regarded the young stranger; and before he had been many months in the house his nightly vigils were the theme of many a serious conversation in the kitchen, where, in front of a cosy fire, the gossips gathered to compare notes.

Unable to repress their vulgar curiosity, or to gratify it in any more honourable or less dangerous manner, it was determined that one of the domestics should, at the hour of twelve, creep to the door of the visitor's chamber, and endeavour to discover what was the nature of those pursuits which rendered lights necessary during the whole of the night. The selection was soon made, and after a little demur the chosen one agreed to perform the unpleasant task.

At midnight, therefore, the trembling ambassador made his way to the distant door, and after a little hesitation, natural enough under the circumstances, he stooped, and gazed through a hole in the dried oak whence a knot had fallen. Edgar Astley was seated at a little table, an old black-looking book with huge clasps open before him. With one hand he shaded his eyes from the light which fell upon his face from the flames of many colours dancing in a tall brazen cup. Suddenly, however, he turned from his book, and put a few pinches of a bright-looking powder to the burning matter in the stand. A searching and sickly odour immediately filled the room, and the quivering flames blazed upwards with increased life and vigour as the student turned once more to the ponderous tome, and, after hastily glancing down its pages, muttered: 'Strange that I cannot yet work the spell. All things named here have I sought for and found, even blood of bat, dead man's hand, venom of viper, root of gallows mandrake, and flesh of unbaptized and strangled babe. Am I, then, not to succeed until I try the charm of charms at the risk of life itself? And yet,' said he, unconscious of the presence of the terrified listener, 'what should I fear? So far have I gone uninjured, and now will I proceed to the triumphant or the bitter end. Once I would have given the future happiness of my soul to have called her by my name, and now what is this paltry life to me that I should hesitate to risk it in this quest, and perhaps win one glimpse of her face?'

There was a moment of silence as the student bent his head over the book, but though no other person was visible, the listener, to his horror, quickly heard a sharp hissing voice ask, 'And wouldst thou not even yet give thy soul in exchange for speech with thy once betrothed?' The student hastily stood erect, and rapidly cried: 'Let me not be deceived! Whatever thou art, if thou canst bring her to me my soul shall be thine now and for ever!'

There was a dead hush for a minute or two, during which the lout at the door heard the beating of his own heart, and then the invisible being again spoke: 'Be it so. Thou hast but one spell left untried. When that has been done thou shalt have thy reward. Beneath the oak at midnight she shall be brought to thee. Darest thou first behold me?'

'I have no fear,' calmly replied the student, but such was not the state of the petrified listener, for no sooner had the lights commenced to burn a weird blue than he sank fainting against the door.

When he came to consciousness he was within the awful room, the student having dragged him in when he fell.

'What art thou, wherefore dost thou watch me at this hour, and what hast thou seen?' sternly demanded Edgar, addressing the terrified boor, and in few and trembling words the unhappy domestic briefly answered the queries; but the student did not permit him to leave the chamber, through the little window of which the dawn was streaming, before he had sworn that not a word as to anything he had seen or heard should pass his lips. The solemnity of the vow was deepened by the mysterious and awful threats with which it was accompanied, and the servant, therefore, loudly protested to his fellows that he had not seen or heard anything, but that, overcome by his patient watching, he had fallen asleep at the door; and many were the congratulations which followed when it was imagined what the consequences would have been had he been discovered in his strange resting-place.

The day following that of the adventure passed over without anything remarkable beyond the absence of Edgar from his usual seat under the shade of the giant oak, but the night set in stormily, dark clouds scudded before the wind, which swept up from the distant sea, and moaned around the old tower, whirling the fallen leaves in fantastic dances about the garden and the green, and shaking in its rage even the iron boughs of the oak. The household had retired early, and at eleven o'clock only Edgar and another were awake. In the student's chamber the little lamp was burning and the book lay open as usual, and Edgar pored over the pages, but at times he glanced impatiently at the quaint clock. At length, with a sigh of relief, he said, sternly and sadly, 'The time draws nigh, and once more we shall meet!' He then gathered together a few articles from different corners of the room and stepped out upon the broad landing, passed down the noble old staircase, and out from the hall. Here he was met by a cold blast of wind, which shrieked round him, as though rejoicing over its prey; and as Edgar was battling with it, a man emerged from a recess and joined him.

The night was quite dark, not a star or a rift in the sky visible, and the two men could hardly pick their way along the well-known path. They reached the oak tree, however, and Edgar placed the materials at its foot, and at once, with a short wand, drew a large circle around the domestic and himself. This done, he placed a little cauldron on the grass, and filled it with a red powder, which, although the wind was roaring through the branches above, immediately blazed up with a steady flame.

The old mastiffs chained under the gateway began to howl dismally; but, regardless of the omen, Edgar struck the ground three times with his hazel stick, and cried in a loud voice: 'Spirit of my love, I conjure thee obey my words, and verily and truly come to me this night!'

Hardly had he spoken when a shadowy figure of a beautiful child appeared, as though floating around the magic ring. The servant sank upon his knees, but the student regarded it not, and it vanished, and the terrified listener again heard Edgar's voice as he uttered another conjuration. No sooner had he begun this than terrible claps of thunder were heard, lightning flashed round the tree, flocks of birds flew across the garden and dashed themselves against the window of the student's chamber, where a light still flickered; and, loud above the noises of the storm, cocks could be heard shrilly crowing, and owls uttering their mournful cries. In the midst of this hubbub the necromancer calmly went on with his incantation, concluding with the dread words: 'Spirit of my love, I conjure thee to fulfil my will without deceit or tarrying, and without power over my soul or body earthly or ghostly! If thou comest not, then let the shadow and the darkness of death be upon thee for ever and ever!'

As the last word left his lips the storm abated its violence, and comparative silence followed. Suddenly the little flame in the cauldron flared up some yards in height, and sweet voices chanting melodiously could be heard. 'Art thou prepared to behold the dead?' asked an invisible being.

'I am!' undauntedly answered Edgar.

An appearance as of a thick mist gathered opposite him, and slowly, in the midst of it, the outlines of a beautiful human face, with mournful eyes, in which earthly love still lingered, could be discerned.

Clad in the garments of the grave, the betrothed of Edgar Astley appeared before him.

For some time the young man gazed upon her as though entranced, but at length he slowly extended his arms as though to embrace the beautiful phantom. The domestic fell upon his face like one stricken by death, the spectre vanished, and again the pealing thunder broke forth.

'Thou art for ever mine,' cried a hissing voice; but as the words broke upon the ears of the two men, the door of the mansion was flung open, and the old baronet and a number of the servants, who had been disturbed by the violence of the storm, the howling of the dogs, and the shrill cries of the birds, rushed forth.

'Come not near me if ye would save yourselves,' cried the necromancer.

'We would save thee,' shouted the old man, still advancing. '*In nomine Patris*,' said he, solemnly, as he neared the magic circle; and no sooner had the words left his lips than sudden stillness fell upon the scene; the lightning no longer flashed round the oak; and, as the flame in the cauldron sank down, the moon broke through a cloud, and threw her soft light over the old garden.

Edgar was leaning against the oak tree, his eyes fixed in the direction where the image of his betrothed had appeared; and when they led him away, it was as one leads a trusting child, for the light of reason had left him. The unfortunate domestic, being less sensitive, retained his faculties; but he ever afterwards bore upon his wrist, as if deeply burned into the flesh, the marks of a broad thumb and fingers. This strange appearance he was wont to explain to stray visitors, by saying that when, terrified almost out of his wits, he fell to the ground, his hand was outside the magic circle, and 'summat' seized him; which lucid explanation was generally followed up by an old and privileged servitor, who remarked, 'Tha'll t'hev mooar marks nor thuse on tha' next toime as *He* grabs tha', mi lad.'

The Black Cock

'Aye,' said Old 'Lijah, 'I remember one time when they said the Owd Lad[4] himself appeared in broad daylight, and was seen by hundreds of folk, old and young.

There was a dead silence for a little while as the listeners gathered nearer the blazing fire, two or three of them getting a little further away from the door, against which the wind was dashing the snow, and then 'Lijah resumed:

'When I was a lad, me and my master were invited to a funeral. There was a lot of drink stirring, sharing the coffee pot, and waiting, until at last it was ready to start. But just as they were beginning to lift the coffin, a clap of thunder shook the very glasses off the table.

The chaps that had hold of the coffin stopped a bit and looked around, but the dead chap's father shouted, "come on lads, or we'll be late and the parson won't bury him." So they set off, but no sooner had they got to the street when a lad in the crowd cried out, "Hey, chaps, look at the black cock on the top of the coffin," and sure enough, there it was.

One of the bearers said directly as they'd enough to carry without any passengers, and lifted up his fist to knock it off, but it was straight back on again. One by one they had a slap at it, but every time it was knocked off, back it flew to its place at the dead man's feet, so at last the old

---

:vil

man gave the word of command, and off they started with the load.

The crowd got bigger before they reached the old country church where he had to be buried, and the folk started throwing stones at the black bird, and hitting it with sticks, and shouting at it, but it stuck there like a permanent fixture.

After a while, we reached the graveyard and the parson came down the road from the church door to meet the coffin, and he was just beginning to start the service when he saw the bird and stopped.

"What have you got there?" he says, looking very vexed, for he thought some mischief was going on. "What have you got there, men?"

The old father stepped forward and told him what had happened, and as none of them could frighten it off its perch, neither with sticks or stones or swearing.

"It's a strange tale," said the vicar, "but we can't have any birds here! You folk keep out of the graveyard anything that isn't invited to the funeral! I'll sort him for you!" and so saying, he grabbed the bird's head, and walked over the graves with it to a place where the brook ran under the hedges, bent down to the ground, and held the birds head under the water for about a quarter of an hour.

No sooner had he got up, however, when the bird flew up out of the water, quite unhurt, and hopped over the grass to the coffin and perched again as if nothing had happened.

The vicar looked very concerned for a while, and scratched his head as he stared at the people.

"There's something not right about that bird," he said, "but that's no reason why we shouldn't bury the dead!" and he pottered off towards the grave, and the bearers carried the coffin to the side, and the service was run through, with the bird listening to every word like a Christian.

The chaps then started to lower the coffin into the grave, with the bird still stuck to its perch, and it wasn't until the hole was filled that it came above ground again, and there it sat on the mound.

A crowd of folk waited about, hanging around the graveyard until dusk and then they set off home, for they began to think that maybe it was the Owd Lad himself, but a few of us stopped until it was night before we followed them, the cock sitting there just the same as it had done in the daylight.

It was usual in those days to watch over the graves for a few nights, for there was a great deal of trouble going on with body snatchers, but though the dead chaps father offered money and plenty of meat and drink to anybody who would keep a look out, no-one dared to do it, and the dead man was left to take care of himself, or for the bird to mind him.

Soon after daylight the next morning, I went with a few more young chaps to see how the place looked. The grave hadn't been broken into, but the bird had flown, and from that day to this, I could never find out where it had come from or gone to, but I heard that the vicar said it must have been the Owd Lad claiming his own.

The Invisible Burden

At the junction of the four cross roads, gleaming white in the hot sunshine and hawthorn-bounded, and marked by the parallel ruts made by the broad wheels of the country carts, the old public house of the *Wyresdale Arms* was scarcely ever without a number of timber wagons or hay carts about its open door, the horses quietly munching from the nose-bags and patiently waiting until their owners or drivers should emerge from the sanded kitchen.

Nathan Peel's hostelry was the half-way house for all the farmers and cart-drivers in the district, and generally quiet enough at night time, but from its capacious kitchen roars of laughter rang out many a summer afternoon, as the carters and yeomen told their droll stories.

On one of these occasions, when the sun was blazing outside, and shimmering upon the sands and the distant sea, and through the open window the perfume of the may-blossom stole gently, a quaint looking old fellow, whose face had been bronzed by three-score summers and winters, happened to mention an occurrence as having taken place about the time of 'the strange wedding,' and a chorus of voices at once called upon him for the story.

'It's quite forty year since,' he said thoughtfully, 'and I was quite a young chap then, and ready for any prank. I could dance too, an' no wedding was complete without inviting me. This one I'm going to tell you about however, was Mister Singleton's oldest son, of Dyke Farm, and he was marrying the prettiest lass in the countryside. Nearly everyone was there, especially as

Mister Singleton had announced that everyone would be welcome.

A convoy of nearly twenty vehicles, milk carts, shandrys[5], and gigs, went to the church with wedding guests, but coming back, young Adam started off with his young wife as if he was mad, and insisted on going the old road across the Stone Bridge, and through the Holme meadow he pelted off through Ingleton Road and Old Horse Lane. The mare seemed to know what he was up to, and he entered into the spirit of the thing and off he went like the wind, the string of shandrys and milk carts and gigs pelting a mile behind them, and the folk laughing and shaking at the fun of it.

The gate into the Old Horse Lane was open, so the folk were disappointed they didn't get a chance to gain a minute or too off their lead. Into the lane the mare dashed, and on they went as if the shandry with Adam and his wife were nothing behind her.

About halfway down the lane, however, the road dipped a bit and the water from a spring ran over it, and just before the shandry reached it, the mare stopped suddenly. Adam flew out over the horse's back and was pitched straight into the hedge. His wife shouted as if he'd been killed, but he'd no bones broken, and when the rest of us caught up with him he crept out of the prickles with a shame faced look as if he'd been caught stealing.

There was some joking around as he climbed up to the side of his wife again and tried to get the mare to start once more, but it was no use, she wouldn't move an inch.

---

[5] A horse drawn cart with sprung suspension.

Adam tried his hardest to get her to move, but it made no difference, so at last eight or ten of us set to and pushed the cart. For twenty or thirty yards it was as though it weighed the same as a fully loaded timber wagon, it was that hard to move. It was the same for every vehicle, not one could be moved through the water without eight or ten of us toiling and slaving at the wheels, no matter how the horses strained and pulled.

Nobody could make out what was happening, and the vicar came to look too, but couldn't find anything wrong. He said, however, that the Owd Lad must have a hand in it, and he warned people not to use the road unless absolutely necessary. Many a time however, I saw carts stuck there after they'd tried the lane as a short cut, or had been dared to try it after a few drinks.

This went on for some years, and folk came from far and near to see it. I'd wed myself and ran a farm on the Holme, but I used to go round the long way whenever I needed to go that way. But one day, a bright, hot day, I'd my little lad in the cart and he'd tried to persuade me to go through the lane, as he wanted to see the Owd Lad he said, and I agreed to do it to stop him crying about it. Well, the cart stuck in the old place by the running water. I got down and took hold of the wheel, for I knew it was no use using the whip, and the horse was sweating as if it was scared senseless, when little Will shouted out all of a sudden, "Father, I can see him!"

"See what?" I shouted out, and broad daylight as it were, my knees were shaking with fear.

"A little chap in the cart," he said, "a fat little chap with a red night cap on."

"Where is he?" I shouted, for I couldn't see owt.

"There on the cart tail," he said, and then he shouted, "Why, he's gone," and no sooner had he spoken than the horse started off with the cart as if it had nothing behind it.

There was never a cart stuck there after that, and the vicar said it was because little Will had seen the Feeorin[6], and that Will must have the gift of seeing Feeorin and the like because he was born at midnight.

---

[6] Fairy folk.

The Boggart in Top Attic

There was a bold lad and his dad's farm was pestered by a boggart that shrieked and whined and thumped and howled outside the top attic window.

"It'll be owls, you see," says he, "I'll drive them off, aye, and I'll sleep in the top attic as well Dad."

His dad said he'd be alright, but his mother she was in a great taking. A notable woman, she was always asking where they'd be without her, but somehow they didn't tell her owt as she'd have wished them to.

So the lad just eased his dad's mind about sending the boggart back where it'd come from, and didn't mention it to his mother. "I'll see and put my best boots under the bed, cobbler has them both new shoe'd with a cross of nails an'all. I reckon two of them heft at him will give him something to howl at and take him off at the double – that is, if he is a boggart – our mother says he isn't, but no need to mention it to her, to come meddling."

"She won't go up attic," said his dad, "She keeps fire lit in the kitchen all night, and we sleep on the settles with candles on the table so it's light as day. Queer sort of taking on, if it's only an owl."

But she *did* go up there at midday while the men were out working.

She had seen him tiptoe up there with his best boots, not asking her, so up she goes at a trot and there were his best boots under the bed. "Thought he'd go wearing them courting down Muck Lane," she said, thinking herself very wise, "I'll teach him! His Sunday wear and just been resoled too! He can traipse around Muck Lane in his ten-year old pair that I was throwing out for the next beggar to come by." So down she went at a run and came back up with the old pair, swapped them over, and came down again at a gallop. "Where'd he be without me?" she says to herself.

When it was time for bed, no-one said owt. The lad went up and his mum and dad bedded down on the kitchen settles with candles, firelight, and all, and the boggart starts up. Then there came two crashes and all went quiet. "That's sorted," says the farmer, and goes to sleep contented.

When morning came there was no lad down to get his porridge, so up his parents went to the attic. There they found no boy, no boots, and they never saw him no more -and where'd he be without his mother's help?

A Cure for Toothache

Someone met an old blacksmith in the village street with his head heavily bandaged. "Now then Arthur," he said, "You don't look too cracking. What's wrong with you?"

"I've been laid up in hospital", he replied.

"Whatever was the matter then?"

"Toothache," said Arthur. "I had raging toothache, so I called to mind what my mother used to do when we were little. She'd get a hammer, make us lay our heads alongside gatepost, then she'd give the top of the post a good sharp crack with the hammer. Either toothache would stop or the bad tooth came out. So it were killing me at the forge, and I called to my apprentice Patrick to bring along a hammer. He's a good fella Patrick, but not the sharpest knife in the drawer, if you know what I mean. You have to be careful about how you explain things to him, careful indeed. So I takes Patrick, shows him the gatepost and hammer, and then I says:

'Now then, Patrick. When I lay my head against the gatepost, you hit it – and that's just what he did!'"

Silken Janet (or Mucketty Meg)

There was a pretty lass they called Jane, but she was proud and greedy and very poor. She thought that her looks made a lady of her and she wouldn't lift a finger to sweep or dust or clean, or even clean herself, or help on the farm, or mind the sheep. She said they were dirty and when they answered her, "dirty beast," she didn't like it.

She wouldn't milk the cows, she said they were mucky and when they answered her with "mucky Minny," she didn't like that either.

As for the pigs, she said they stank and when they answered, "stinking slut[7]," she liked it no better.

One day she stole some silk from a ladies' bower on the fairy knoll and made herself a fine gown to wear over her old rags, but she didn't bother to wash. The she went back to walk on the fairy knoll, so when they saw her on *their* land in all her dirt and stolen finery, they had a mind to punish her.

So all the beasts began to call out to her:

Silken Janet she wears a fine gown,

She stole it, she stole it from Down-a-down.

She never paid a penny,

---

[7] I should note here that the common meaning of slut used to be someone "with low standards of cleanliness" rather than someone with many sexual partners.

Because she hadn't any.

They made such a racket that people heard and they caught Silken Janet. They were going to take away the silk dress, but it was so dirty they said she should be hanged in it instead for stealing. Then she cried out to the beasts to help her, but they all answered:

Nobody likes a grimy lass,

Nobody wants a slut, a slut,

Nobody wants a dirty beast,

Go away and roll in the muck.

Well, she couldn't get away and roll in anything, even if she'd wanted to.

Then she shouted out to the lads, "will you not help a pretty lass?", but then they answered her:

Nobody likes a grimy lass,

Nobody wants a slut, a slut,

Nobody wants a dirty beast,

Go away and roll in the muck.

She couldn't anyway, and the hangman had got the rope around her neck by now. She saw a fine gentleman in green and called out to him, "will you not save a pretty lass?" and he said, "Leave it with me, but you must pay me your two blue eyes."

"What will I see with?" she begged.

"Green ones," said he, taking away her blue ones and leaving her with green. Well, she cried, but the rope was still there. "I'll give you my fine golden gown," she said.

"It's stolen! I'll not touch that. I want real gold," he said.

"I have none!" She cried.

"There's all your pretty gold hair under the dirt, I'll take that," and he cut it all off. "Now go and wash in the river." She got out of the rope and ran away from the crowd so fast that she fell straight in the river when she got there.

When she climbed out she cried over the loss of her golden tresses of hair. But nobody came to hang her, and when she looked down at herself she saw that the golden dress had been washed off too, with her rags sparkling clean.

Then the pig came by, "Good morning, clean lass," said he.

Then a sheep came by, "Pretty, clean, curly locks," said she. And she put up her hand to her newly short hair and saw it was clean and curly.

Then a cow came by with a pail on her horns, "I'll let you milk me, my clean, pretty lass," she said, "there's a crowd looking for a dirty, golden slut that was to be hanged, and I don't want them to have my milk."

So she set to milking, and she did it quite well too. When the crowd came by, she kept her face hidden against the cow. But the gentleman in green took her by the hair and looked at her. "This is a clean lass!" he said, "she's got a lint-white, linen gown, and curly, link-white locks. But she's got *green eyes*." They were so disappointed; they threw her in the river again.

When she climbed out this time, she couldn't see any of the crowd, or the gentleman in green, or the gallows. She was all in her washed rags and her long golden hair hung down to dry about her, and she was back on the fairy knoll.

"I best be out of here", she said, and ran for home. She ran until her dry rags fluttered in the wind and her golden hair streamed about her, when she ran into a young farmer.

"Good morning, blue eyes," he said, "I'm looking for a clean, pretty wife to work all her days. Will you marry me?"

"That I will, gladly," said Silken Janet.

Dule upon Dun

In his Rambles on the Ribble[8] Mr. Dobson records what professes to be a genuine Lancashire tale which has been told for generations by many a fireside on the banks of that river.

There stood till recently in the town of Clitheroe a public-house bearing the strange name of Dule upon Dun, on the signboard of which the devil was depicted riding off at full speed upon a dun horse, while a tailor, scissors in hand, looked on with delight.

It appears that in former days, when the Evil One used to visit the earth in bodily form and enter into contracts with mortals, giving them material prosperity now in exchange for the soul at a future time, a tailor of Clitheroe entered into some such agreement with him.

At the expiration of the term, however, the tailor having failed to receive any benefit at all from the agreement, asked from his Satanic Majesty the boon of "one wish more." It was granted. A dun horse was grazing hard by, and the ready-witted tailor, pointing to the animal, wished that the devil might ride straight to his own quarters upon it and never come back to earth to plague mortal man. Instantly the horse was bestridden by the Evil One, who speedily rode out of sight never to return in a bodily shape.

People came from far and near to see the man who had outwitted the devil, and soon it occurred to the tailor to

---

[8] An 1864 book.

set up an alehouse for the entertainment of his visitors, taking for a sign the devil riding a dun horse, or as the neighbours called it for brevity "the Dule[9] upon Dun."

---

[9] Devil

Nut Nan and more...[10]

Nuts were plentiful in our forefathers' days; they were to be met with in the hedges enclosing every field and lane, and especially in the cloughs, and near brook sides. Few hazels are now to be found, and fewer still which are nuciferous. To deter children from gathering the fruit before it was ripe, they terrified their young imaginations by awful accounts of a demoness, the guardian of young catkins, nuts, and nut trees; she bore the classic title of 'Nut Nan.' Her office was to seize children who purloined nuts before they were ripe. Some affirmed she had 'a poke full o'red whot yettors, to brun nut staylurs wee.[11]'

In conjunction with her were associated Clapcans, who made a loud jarring noise by beating cans with sticks. To restrain their children from venturing too near the numerous pits and pools which were to be found in every fold and field, a demoness or guardian was stated to crouch at the bottom. She was known as 'Jenny Greenteeth,' and was reported to prey upon children who ventured too near her domain. Sometimes the water demoness was termed 'Grindylow.'

Many an old country dame, when nursing a boisterous fretful child or grandchild, has endeavoured to frighten it

---

[10] From John Higson, *The Gorton Historical Recorder*, (Droylsden: Privately printed, 1852)

[11] A pocket or bag full of red hot heaters to burn little nut stealers.

into quietness or obedience by repeating loudly, with a somewhat mysterious and vacant look, some such phrase as 'Will wit' whisp, Jack weet lanturn, un Peg weet iron teeth.[12,]

---

[12] This is Peg Powler, similar to Jenny Greenteeth but from the river Tees.

The Devil and the Tailor

There was a tailor in our town,

Who was a worthy wight;

All through the day

He worked away,

And half way through the night.

He had a wife who he did love,

And he had children bright;

To find the meat

For them to eat,

Did puzzle the tailor quite.

One day as on the board he sat,

When cupboard and shelf were bare,

The children cried,

Unsatisfied

With feeding on the air.

Oh! Then unto himself he said,

"Ah! Would that I were rich,

With meat galore,

And money in store,

And never a coat to stitch."

"If Old Nick now to me would say,

'in riches you may roll',

I'm sure I'd sell

To the Lord of Hell

Myself, both body and soul."

The Devil unto the tailor came,

And thus to him said he,

"The bag of gold,

Is wealth untold,

And emptied ne'er shall be.

Exhaustless is its boundless store,

And it shall all be thine

Whilst thou has breath,

But at thy death

Thy soul shall then be mine."

"Nay, put the matter as a bet,

Thy bag against my soul;

We each will take

A coat to make,

The quickest to take the whole."

Old Nick to this at once agreed,

And thought the tailor to wheedle;

"My sight is bad,

So I'll be glad,

If you would thread my needle."

"A needleful I'll put you in,"

The tailor said, "with pleasure,

Sound and true,

To last all through,

The job we are to measure."

A needleful he put him in,

The tailor did with pleasure,

Sound and true,

To last all through,

A hundred yards by measure.

To work the two men did settle then;

The tailor worked in dread;

The devil flew

The room all through,

With his hundred yards of thread.

But though the Devil beat his wings,

And panted fit to burst,

With shorter thread,

And clearer head,

The tailor finished first.

Thus was the Devil overcome,

And fairly left i'the lurch;

The tailor wight,

Became a knight,

And always went to church.

He patronised charities,

And never joined a revel;

To end my song,

I think it's wrong,

To swindle – e'en the Devil.

Fairest of all others

A poor fisherman found a floating box with a baby girl inside. He took it home to his wife and they agreed together they'd rear the baby as their own, even though they were eighty and seventy five years old.

People came from all over to see the marvel of this baby found at sea, among them a squire's son who offered to read her future in a horoscope. Surprised to find she was destined to marry him, he became determined to stop it. He told the old couple he'd be happy to adopt her and give her a life of luxury, but just as importantly, make sure she could be looked after bearing in mind the couple's advanced age.

They agreed the squire's son could take her, and he gave them £200 for their trouble. Once she was handed over, however, he had a box made, cut a large cross on the baby's cheek with his knife to mark her forever, put it in the box and threw it into the sea.

Luckily, the very same fisherman found the box and took the baby home once more. She was brought up until she was seventeen, a beautiful young woman despite the scar on her cheek. As the squire's son was riding through the area he heard of this girl with a cross shaped scar and realised it must be the same person as the baby he had thrown into the sea so many years before.

He came to her house when she was home along, and unrecognised, hired her to be cook at his grand home on condition she left with him immediately. On the way back he stopped at a lonely spot on the coast and drew out his sword to kill her. She begged for her life, and he relented on one condition. He took a ring from his finger and threw it into the sea, saying that if he ever saw her again he would kill her unless she returned that ring to him. He rode off home, leaving her at the coast alone.

She walked off looking for shelter and work, too far to return home on foot. A lady took her in and engaged her as her cook. While there she became famous for her cooking skills and her beauty, becoming known as the "Fairest of All Others". Whenever people visited the lady, they would also ask to see the beautiful cook. One day she'd bought some fish and was preparing them for visitors who were expected that evening. Inside one of them she found the ring that had been thrown into the sea, so she cleaned in and kept hold of it.

As the guests arrived, they demanded to see the "Fairest of All Others", so she was called up from the kitchen to meet them. One was the Squire's son, who drew his sword immediately to kill her, recognising her, and her scar, immediately. She produced the ring and reminded him of what he had said on the beach. At that, he finally submitted to fate, and married her as soon as it could be arranged. They had many fine sons and fair daughters.

The Clever Little Tailor

Three children, two brothers and a sister, had promised their father to always keep together and look after one another. They heard about a festivity that was happening nearby, so went together, but found nothing there. Slightly confused, they looked around, and the elder brother spotted a light. The boys ran towards the light but found nothing, but returned to find their sister missing and signs that she had been carried away.

They followed the trail but it seemed to disappear into the ground. Determined not to lose their sister, they dug down into a subterranean land, where they found that she had been abducted by a two headed giant who wanted to marry her. She hid her brothers when they arrived at the giant's house, but was forced to reveal them before they could get away to safety. He blackmailed her into marrying him, threatening to kill her brothers if she did not.

The giant tolerated the brothers for a while, but disliked the younger one intently. One day he took the younger brother to the seaside, had him beaten, stripped, tied down, and covered so he was unrecognisable. He then tricked his wife into blinding her own brother with red-hot irons, and left him to die on the beach. Some monkeys took pity on him, untying him and carrying him to a "high institution" where the blind and sick were healed. They nursed him back to health, but could not heal his blindness, though he dreamed regularly of a well that would cure his blindness if only he could find it.

The giant, perhaps to remind his wife of what she had done, visited the "high institution" regularly with his wife. The blind brother asked them for their help in finding the well, but the giant dismissed it as nonsense, saying that no such place existed. With his sister's help, however, he found the well on an island just off the coast, and was cured. With his sight restored, he set off from the island and tried to find work in his old trade as tailor.

He visited the house of another giant who didn't need a tailor, but set him to farm work instead, as they needed someone to do the finer work that a smaller person could do better than a giant. The giant's wife was frightened of humans though, and persuaded her husband to kill him while he slept at night with his club. He overheard this plan, putting a calf in his place. The giants were more scared then ever the next morning, thinking he'd survived being flattened by the giant's club.

When the tailor heard of a local challenge being held by the giants, he went along and challenged the ogre who had married his sister to an eating contest. He'd stitched a bag under his jacket in advance, however, and secretly poured the majority of the food down into the bag while the giant ate. As the giant became full and slowed his eating, the tailor announced that he was nearly full so must make space! He took out his knife and pretended to cut open his stomach, though of course only cut into the bag full of food. He then carried on eating, telling everyone he was sure to win now. Determined not to be beaten, the giant cut open his own stomach, quickly dying from the injury.

With his wife and brother now free, the three of them took all they could carry from the giant's house and returned home safely.

The Bottle of Water from the World's End Well

A King's daughter had a cruel stepmother, who set her menial tasks that seemed impossible to do. One day she told her to draw water with a sieve. While she was struggling to work out how she could do it, a frog advised her to stop the holes with moss and clay, so she managed to fill and carry it back to her stepmother.

The next day, she was tasked with washing some black wool white. Nothing she did made a difference until a bird advised her to go to a particular spring, dip it in and wring it three time. That she did, and it turned white before her very eyes.

The day after she was given a bottle and told to fill it at the well at the world's end. She set off to find it, but on the way came across a shaggy pony tied to a tree. The pony asked her to free it, and in return it agreed to carry her to the well. It was too deep for her to dip the bottle in, however, and she had no rope to lower it in with. While she was struggling, three dirty heads popped up out of the well! They asked her to wash and brush them and in return they would fill the bottle. She did such a good job of washing and brushing them that they not only filled the bottle, they gave her three blessings: An increase in her beauty, a voice like silver bells, and gold that fell out of her hair whenever she brushed it. She went home with the bottle and everyone was amazed by her blessings.

The stepmother was annoyed and sent her own daughter to get the same benefits. This girl refused to untether the pony, so had to walk all the way to the world's end and back. She refused to wash and brush the three heads, so they cursed her with being: ten times uglier, that dirt should drop from her mouth whenever she spoke, and that she should get a quart pot of lice whenever she combed her hair.

The stepsister returned home in disgrace and was turned out of the palace, married off to an ugly beggar man. The lovely princess married a great King's son, while her stepmother died in despair.

Lousy Jack and his Eleven Brothers

An old woman had twelve sons. The youngest, Jack, was lousy[13] and despised by everyone. The time came for them all to set off and seek their fortunes, so they started out together until they got to a point where twelve roads met. Each took a different road, agreeing to meet again after a year and a day.

Jack went along the dirtiest road, travelling for many months until he reached a castle with a golden phoenix over the door. As he approached the door, the phoenix said "If you venture into this castle, you will see things that make your blood run cold."

Lousy Jack went in despite the warning, finding it full of animals and people stood frozen in place like statues. He explored all over the castle until he reached a dark cellar stack full with a pile of thorns. He was so lousy that he enjoyed the scratching of the thorns, burrowing into them until he bumped into a figure buried at the centre of them. It was an enchanted princess, and his touch broke the spell – a light went on in the cellar and the princess moved.

Jack pulled the thorns away from her, and when they came out of the cellar all the frozen people and animals were alive and working. Lousy Jack told the princess that he had found her accidentally, rather than trying to rescue her, but she was so pleased to have been saved she was ready to marry him. He welcomed this, but said he had to

---

[13] Literally, infected by lice!

return to meet his brothers again first and set off immediately.

So he set off back to the crossroads and met them all a year and a day after first separating. He told them all he'd rescued a princess under a pile of thorns, but not in great detail before they threw him into a ditch, intending that one of them could claim the princess themselves.

They made their way along the dirty road until they found the castle, with the oldest telling the princess that he was the brother who rescued her. He told her the story of how he found her under the thorns, but he didn't know that it was accidental, so the princess saw through his story. All eleven of the brothers tried and were rejected, as none of them had heard the full story from lousy Jack.

The Princess proclaimed that she would wed her true rescuer, and Jack, after escaping from the ditch, heard it, coming to claim her. He married the Princess and became King, living in the grand castle... but he was lousy all his days.

The Man Who Didn't Believe in Ghosts and 'chantments

There was a poor man who didn't believe in ghosts or enchantments of any sort. A friend told him of an enchanted house nearby and challenged him to stop overnight in it, to see if he still thought the same afterwards. It was owned by a local squire who had been driven out by the enchantments on the house, building himself another home nearby – he welcomed them trying to stay over and warned them they might not manage it.

As they explored the house, they went into a fine dining room, with a bare table, and they agreed it would be finer still if it was full of food for their dinner! To their surprise food floated into the room and set itself down on the table before them. They sat down to eat, and as they finished the table magically cleared itself, with pipes and tobacco appearing instead.

They were beginning to think that this was a fine place to stay when they heard an uproar upstairs. They went off to investigate and met a man in football kit who advised them to go to bed if they wanted to be safe. So they checked out the bedrooms, and were just settling into the comfortable beds when they heard an uproar downstairs. They went down to check out what was happening and found a football match in full flow, though no-one seemed to really know what they were doing. The unbeliever joined in and kicked the ball clean through one of the windows. At this, the ghosts turned on them and threw them both out of the house.

They lay stunned in the gardens for a few moments, then went back towards the house. Through the windows they could see a party of figures in evening dress watching a play, but when they entered the house, they all vanished.

Well, the two men were confused rather than scared, and began to think it might be nice to see if they could get supper in the same way as their dinner earlier. They looked through the house, wishing for a bite of something to eat, when a ghost appeared in front of them and told them he would bring them some. Plate after plate of food he brought it, but each time he got close to the men he scoffed down every morsel himself. At last the unbeliever got angry, grabbed an empty plate, and smashed it over the ghost's head.

This broke the enchantment and the ghost disappeared – they heard and saw no more commotion during the night, nor the next morning. No breakfast was magically conjured for them either. When they told the squire that the house was safe once more, he was so pleased he gifted them the house to stay in, as he thought that he'd lost it anyway.

The Dragon of Wantley

This dragon was the terror of all the countryside. He had forty-four iron teeth, and a long sting in his tail, besides his strong rough hide and fearful wings.

He ate trees and cattle, and once ate three young children at one meal. Fire breathed from his nostrils, and for a long time no man dared to come near to him.

Near to the dragon's den, there lived a strange knight names More of More Hall. It was said that he was so strong that he had once seized a horse by its mane and tail, and swung it round and round until it was dead, because it had angered him. Then, said the tale, he had eaten the horse – all except its head.

At last the people terrorised by the dragon came together to More Hall and with tears implored the knight to free them from the terrible monster, which was devouring all their food, and making them fear for their very lives. They offered him all their remaining goods if he would do them this service.

But the knight accepted nothing, but asked instead for one black-haired maid of sixteen to anoint him for the battle at night, and array him, in his armour in the morning. When they promised him this, he went to Sheffield, and found a smith to make him a new set of armour. This was set all over with iron spikes, each five or six inches in length.

Then he made his way to the where the dragon lived, hiding in a well where the dragon had been spotted drinking regularly. As it stooped to the water, the knight popped up with a shout and struck it a full blow in the

face. But the dragon was straight upon him, hardly
slowed by the initial blow, and for two days and two
nights they fought without either inflicting a wound on
the other. At last, the dragon flung itself at More with the
intention of tossing him high into the air. More moved to
the side at just the right moment and planted a kick in the
middle of its back. This was the vital spot, one of the iron
spikes on the armour drove into the monster's flesh so
far that it spun round and round in agony, groaning and
roaring fearfully, but in a few more minutes it was over, it
collapsed into a helpless heap, and died.

Dildrum, King of the Cats

The following tradition is often heard in South Lancashire.

A gentleman was sitting cosily in his parlour one evening, reading or meditating, when he was interrupted by the appearance of a cat, which came down his chimney, and called out "Tell Dildrum, Doldrum's dead!", before disappearing as quickly as it came.

He was naturally startled by this, and when his wife entered shortly afterwards, told her what had happened. His own cat, who had come in with his wife, exclaimed, "Is Doldrum dead? Then I must now be king!" and immediately rushed up the chimney, to be seen or heard of no more.

Of course, there were numberless conjectures upon such a remarkable event, but the general opinion seems to be that Doldrum had been king of the cats, and that Dildrum was the next in line to the throne.

A Fairy Changeling

Pyramus Gray and his wife, Milly Herne, had a four-month old baby named Potamus. One day Milly was working outdoors, and left the baby on a patch of grass nearby, close enough to hear if it cried, but not within sight at all times. The next day she went out begging with the baby strapped to her back, but when she got home she found its pinny was full of nuts and cakes. She had no idea where they had come from, but the same thing happened day after day, and Milly started to fear it was a fairy child.

One day, crossing a river, she slipped off a stepping stone and fell into the water up to her waist. She shouted out in surprise, "Oh dear, we shall be drowned!" The four-month old child looked up to Milly's face and replied "Oh no, Mammy, we shan't!" Her blood ran cold, as she was then sure it was a fairy that had been swapped for her own child.

Milly talked to Pyramus that night and they decided they must go to the parson for advice. He told her to spank the child until it cried, lay it on the ground, then hide out of sight behind a bush for a quarter of an hour. When she came back, the baby was black and blue with bruises, but it was her own child once more. There were no more cakes and nuts, and the baby did not speak until it had reached the right age to do so.

A Fairy Experience

Taimi was wandering along a green lane one evening, when he came upon a tiny tent only about two feet high. It had a fire burning outside it, and a little man eighteen inches or so high, in knee breeches, top boots, a red waistcoat, and a green and yellow neckerchief. They talked, and the man's little wife joined them, wearing a red dress, and with black ringlets.

Taimi admired a small box they had with a pretty doll lying inside it, and offered to buy it from them. They wouldn't take any money, but gave it to him instead. They also gave him another box, with dainty doll's clothes inside.

Pleased with meeting these little people, and with the gifts they had given him, he bade them farewell. As he left, the woman gave him bread, milk, and a little spoon for the doll too, and would accept no refusal. Soon Taimi found himself walking along with a tiny girl on either side of him. One told him she was the doll from the box, and the other that she'd come to keep her company. He tried in vain to get rid of them, as he dared not take them home to his wife, but was forced to sleep under the hedge with one of them on either side of him.

The next morning, when they still refused to go, he tried to throw them into a lily-pond, but they clung to his legs with a strength he wouldn't expect from their size. He began to curse and swear at them, at which point they vanished.

His wife was so angry at his lateness when he arrived home, that he told her the full story. When she wouldn't believe him, he tried to take her to the fairy encampment.

Unfortunately, when they arrived it had disappeared, so she did not believe him. Searching for any evidence that they'd been there before, the realised the tent had been pitched in the middle of a fairy ring, which he'd failed to spot in the twilight the night before. This explained his strange experience.

The Goodwife of Deloraine

The farmer's wife of Deloraine engaged a tailor, his
workmen, and his apprentices for the day, begging them
to come in good time for the morning. They did so, and
partook of the family breakfast of porridge and milk
before they started work. During the meal, one of the
apprentices mentioned that the milk-jug was almost
empty, so the mistress slipped out of the back door with
a basin to get a fresh supply. The lad was curious, as he'd
heard that there was no more milk in the house, so he
crept after her, peering out from behind the door to
watch. He saw her turn a pin in the wall, which made a
stream of pure milk flow into the basin. She twirled the
pin, and the milk stopped. Coming back, she presented
the tailors with the bowl of milk, and they finished their
breakfast with it.

About noon, while the tailors were busily engaged
making clothes for the household, one of them
complained they were thirsty and wished they could have
a glass of milk like they had earlier that morning. "Is that
all?" said the apprentice, "I'll get it." The mistress was
nowhere to be seen, so he left his work, found his way to
the spot he'd seen that morning, and twirled the pin like
he'd seen her do before. The milk flowed once more,
quickly filling the basin in his hand, but alas! He couldn't
stop the stream. Twist the pin as much as he did, the milk
still continued to flow. He called the other lads, begging
them to help him, but all they could do was bring more
buckets and tubs as they could find, which soon filled.

With all the containers full, and milk pouring on the
ground, the mistress appeared amongst them, looking
black as thunder, calling out to them in a mocking voice:

"You loons! You've drawn the milk from every cow from the head of the Yarrow to the foot of it. This day no cow will give her master a drop of milk, even if he's starving for it." The tailors slunk away ashamed of what they'd done, and from that day forward the wives of Deloraine have fed their tailors on nothing but chappit 'taties[14] and kale.

---

[14] Mashed potato with spring onion or chives.

Loynd in the Vale of Todmorden[15]

Giles Robinon, a struggling farmer was wearily travelling through the Vale of Todmorden, heading towards Burnley, hoping to reach his home in Pendle Forest before nightfall. As he walked along the lonely and rugged path, a flash of light passed before his eyes, and immediately after a crash, striking him with amazement. The first idea that came to his mind was that he had been beset by robbers.

Recovering slightly from the initial shock, he looked up to his left and saw a sight that all but smote him to the ground with dismay. It was Loynd, the witch, whose name was a terror throughout the forest of Blackburnshire. Before he could look around again, he found himself in a terrible storm. The thunder roared and echoed on all sides, the rain fell in torrents. Poor Giles was near collapsing of fatigue and dread, when he felt something hard and smooth rub against his legs. Looking down he saw a huge black cat, whose eyes emitted sparks of fire. Suddenly, a voice came forth, as if from his mouth, "You cursed my mistress two days ago, she will meet you again at Malkin Tower." The familiar disappeared, darting more quickly than thought to the top of the precipice above, alighting on the shoulder of Loynd, who was sitting aside "Eagle's Crag." The moment the cat had taken his place, the witch drew a huge burning torch from the beak of the eagle, and waving it around and around, flew away as swiftly and

---

[15] This story is from, "The Vale of Todmorden – the Boggart" in The Leeds Times, April 30th 1842, but shortened slightly.

securely as if she was an eagle herself, in a North-West direction.

"True enough," ejaculated Giles, "she is gone to Pendle Forest. Horrid scenes, doubtless, will take place before the sun in high in the heavens."

On the previous evening, Giles' son had left his home, and wandered forth in an idle mood. Meeting a neighbour, he asked of him to go and gather berries in his small enclosure. Obtaining permission, he darted into the thicket, and was soon lost from sight. After proceeding a few hundred yards, he saw two greyhounds come running towards him over the next field. They approached him and fawned on him, and then he saw with astonishment that their collars were made of gold. Gratified at so fine an opportunity, he determined to hunt with them. Most opportunely, a hare at that moment rose just in front. "Loo! Loo!" he shouted, but not a step would the animals take. He was naturally enraged, and hit the hounds with his cudgel. This stick had a miraculous effect, for instead of the dogs, he now saw Moll Dickenson, and a young boy. Ned, Giles' son, tried to run, but the woman put her hand on his shoulder and he seemed pinned to the ground. "Here," she said, offering him a piece of silver, "take this and hold your peace."

"Anoint thee witch!" replied Ned, "do you think I don't know you?" On which Moll took some string from her pocket and threw it over the boy's neck. At once, he turned into a white horse. Poor Ned felt himself the next moment astride the horse, seated in front of the witch.

Before he recovered from his surprise, he found they had arrived at a new house called Hoarestones, higher up the mountain. The door was beset with beings human in shape, but demonical in aspect. Others were coming up on fiery horses from all around, but in greatest numbers from the Cliviger side of the county. Ned had heard of the "witches sabbath", and was now convinced he was about to witness the horrors of one.

Three score hags crowded the place. They first prepared a feast. At a word, fires were kindled, and whole carcasses roasting before them. Before he could turn his eyes to the table, the meat was already cooked and ready for the carver's knife. Not two minutes passed from the start of the feast when they all arose together, as if at a secret signal, and the one who had brought him there shrieked "feed him! Feed the wretch!" A young comely woman tripped up to him with a delicious steak in a golden dish. Ned's eyes glistened and his mouth watered. He took a bite and was instantly overcome with disgust. Before he knew it, he was astonished to find himself in a barn! Six nags knelt in front of him and pulled on six ropes fastened to the roof. Down from the roof immediately fell roasted lambs, lumps of butter, and the richest cream, falling into dishes and basins placed to catch them. These witches were soon replaced by six more, who continued their work. All around, a hideous cacophony sounded, as if from twelve broken church bells, while owls hooted from hidden corners of the barn, and shrieks and groans sounded from outside.

All of a sudden, a vast cauldron rose upon the barn floor, surrounded both inside and out by lurid and scorching flames. A number of the foulest hags appeared, who, acting under the instructions of one he recognised as Loynd, threw various things into the cauldron as they said:

1st Witch, "Here's the blood of a bat"

Loynd, "Put in that, o put in that"

188

2nd Witch, "Here's Libbard's Bane"

Loynd, "Put in again"

1st Witch, "The juice of toad, the oil of adder"

2nd Witch, "That will make the yonker[16] madder"

Loynd, "Put in, there's all, and rid the stench"

Firestone, "Nay, here's three ounces of the red-hair'd wench"

All, "Round, around, around"

"It takes!" they all suddenly shrieked. "Her flesh has done it!" On which the trembling boy saw his father and mother rise in the opposite corner of the room.

"Wretches!" exclaimed Loynd, "we know and can punish our enemies. You are here to see the fate of your own boy…" but before the sentence was finished, Ned had darted from the barn and hurried towards his home as fast as he could run. He was sure that if he could only get passed the "boggart-hole" he would be safe. The troop of witches, led by Loynd, chased after him.

She was nearly on his heels, and reached out her bony hand to grab him, when he leaped like a wounded deer and full two yards further down the mountain than the boggart hole. That moment, two horsemen came up, the witches scampered into the forest, and Ned was conducted to his home. For a whole week the poor boy did nothing but rave. His father arrived a short time after

---

[16] Young lad

Ned, and found that one object of the gathering of witches had indeed been to punish their household.

For days did Giles remain unemployed, and almost speechless, plotting revenge, until at last he decided to resort to the law. Eighteen persons were brought to trial in Lancaster, seventeen of whom were found guilty on the oath of Giles and his son, and condemned to death. The judge, however, granted the prisoners a reprieve and reported the case to the King at council. The Bishop at Chester examined the case, and four of them were sent to London to be examined by the king's physicians, and afterwards by Charles I in person.

Suspicions arose, Giles and his son were subjected to a very searching investigation, and it was decided that whether or not the father had been scared by a thunderstorm or a witch, the son had been pressured to give a false testimony to serve as an instrument of revenge. That said, one of the accused, Margaret Johnson, had actually confessed her guilt, explaining in detail how, when, where, and for what purpose that she had chosen to become a witch of her own free will.

The Barcroft Boggart[17]

It is said that the farmer's wife at Barcroft on rising in the morning would often find the house clean swept, the fire lighted, other household matters attended to by unseen hands.

One cold winter's night the farmer called out from his bedroom to his son to rise and fetch in the sheep into the barn for shelter, when a small squeaking voice called up the stairs, "I'll do it!" After a short time the small voice was again heard, crying out, "I've done it! But there was a little brown one that gave me more trouble than all the others!"

On examination the following morning, the farmer found that a fine hare had been housed with the sheep. Mortal eyes had as yet never seen the boggart who had proved himself so useful to the household, till the farmer's son, filled with curiosity to see him, bored a hole through the oaken boards of the ceiling above the chamber where the boggart appeared. Peeping through the hole early one morning he saw a little shrivelled old man, barefooted, sweeping up the floor.

Thinking to perform an act of kindness, the boy got a pair of small clogs made for the old man, and placing them by the fireside at night, he rose early in the morning

---

[17] This seems to pop up in various places, but I *think* it's from Memories of Hurstwood Lancashire (1889), by Tattersall Wilkinson – I haven't found the original though to check!

on purpose to look through the hole and see how his well-meant gift was accepted.

The elf walked up to the clogs and took them in its hand, and looking at them carefully, it said, "New clogs, new wood, T'hob Thurs will never do any more good!".

After this everything went wrong in the household. Mischief of every kind was found each morning - pots broken - cows sick - and, to crown all, the bull was found across the ridging of the house when the farmer rose early one morning for his day's work.

His patience gave way at this last signal proof of the boggart's malevolence, and packing up his goods, he determined to leave the luckless house. Having loaded a cart with furniture, he proceeded on his way across a small bridge at the bottom of the clough, when he heard a small voice from beneath calling out, "Stop while I've tied my clogs, and I'll go with you!"

"Nay!" replied the farmer; "If you're going with me, I'll go back again!"

Halstead Changeling[18]

A woman living at High Halstead, a farm near the Roggerham Gate Inn, near Burnely, went to bring some water from the well. In doing so, she was obliged to leave her child asleep in the cot for a few moments.

When she returned her offspring had been replaced by a wizened old thing that looked as "false as a boggart". The poor woman tried everything she could think of to try and regain her child.

In desperation she sought out the advice of a wise old man, who told her that the thing she was holding in her hands, was in fact a fairy changeling. In order to test it, she was told she would have to do some strange and unusual acts to try and get its attention. Eager to regain her child she went home.

She took an empty eggshell which she placed in the fire and poured in some cold water. The wizened changeling looked on all the while with apparent interest. When the water came to the boil and the creature said "what are you going to do with that". She replied "I'm going to make a brew". The changeling cried out in a shrill little voice saying "Well, I'm three score and ten, and I've never seen that done before".

With that the mother snatched up the creature saying "if you're three score and ten, then you leave this house at once".

---

[18] Another one I'm not sure of where it came from originally, but I've seen repeated in a few places!

She then took the changeling out of the house down the meadow to the stream with the cries of the creature resounding through the valley. Suddenly she heard another sound of the crying, which as a mother recognised as that of her own child.

Tracing where the sound was coming from, she found her youngster in the hands of a very old woman who was holding it with all her might. On meeting, they exchanged their children, no words were spoken, but each overjoyed at having regained their own child.

Alderman & Alphin[19]

In Greenfield, on either sides of the valley, lived two giants called Alderman and Alphin. Nearby in a hollow of the moors, near Holme Moss, there lived a beautiful shepherdess called Rimmon. She was fair, tall, and most lovable. She had no extravagent tastes and cared little for fine clothes, often even going about quite naked, with nothing but a bit of heather in her hair.

In Rimmon Clough, which runs down to Sail Bark, there is a pool where she used to bathe on summer mornings, before walking through the long grass and bracken while she dried before getting dressed once more.

The sight of her shapely figure walking naked across the moor drove Alphin and Alderman to fall madly in love with her.

Rimmon flirted with both, enjoying the attention, before making her mind up to smile and blow kisses at Alphin, giving Alderman the cold shoulder. The two giants at once fell out with each other over the shepherdess, arguing and insulting one another.

One morning, through the mist, he caught Alphin embracing and kissing the lady Rimmon. Alderman flew into a jealous rage, damning them both in the ripest

---

[19] This is adapted from "Saddleworth Superstitions and Folk Customs" by Ammon Wrigley, so around the borders of Yorkshire and Lancashire, but it didn't make it into the "Yorkshire" book of tales, so here it is!

language, but the lovers laughed at him and embraced again.

Alderman stormed off to his hill side, rolled up his sleeves, and hurled a great mass of rock at Alphin. These were returned with interest, with Rimmon encouraging her lover, from a safe distance, to fling several tons of stone back at him. Huge rocks and boulder were flung back and forth, until one huge rock knocked the life out of poor Alphin.

Alderman came straight to woo Rimmon, despite just killing her lover. He called her nice names, praising her beauty, her eyes, her waist, her ankles, and more… He promised her all manners of gifts and asked her to sit on his knee.

Rimmon was understandably furious and not at all open to his advances. She spat in his face, called him "too ill to brun", and all the names under the sun. As her initial anger was spent, her grief took over and she began to weep and wail over her dead Alphin. In despair and grief, she threw herself down a precipice, ending her life.

Alderman returned to his his hillside and to this day glowers at his dead rival on the other side of the valley, as they both slowly petrified to stone over the passing years.

Main Sources

From "Goblin Tales of Lancashire", James Bowker, 1883:

- Th' Skriker
- The Unbidden Guest
- The Fairy's Spade
- The King of the Fairies
- Mother and Child
- The Spectral Cat
- The Captured Fairies
- The Pillion Lady
- The Fairy Funeral
- The Chivalrous Devil
- The Enchanted Fisherman
- The Sands of Cocker
- The Silver Token
- The Headless Woman
- The Rescue of Moonbeam
- The White Dobbie
- The Little Man's Gift
- Satan's Supper
- The Earthenware Goose
- The Phantom of the Fell
- Allhallow's Night
- The Christmas Eve Vigil
- The Crier of Claife
- The Demon of the Oak
- The Black Cock
- The Invisible Burden

From "Forgotten Folk Tales of the English Counties",
Ruth Tongue, 1970:

- The Boggart in Top Attic
- A Cure for Toothache
- Silken Janet (or Mucketty Meg)

From "Folktales of England", Katherine Briggs and Ruth
Tongue, 1965:

- Mossycoat

From "Notes on the folk-lore of the northern counties of
England and the Borders", William Henderson, 1879.

- Dule upon Dun (which says it was originally
  from Rambles on the Ribble, 1864, Dobson)

From "A dictionary of British Folk-tales", Katherine
Briggs, 1970.

- The devil and the tailor
- Fairest of all others
- The clever little tailor
- The bottle of water from the world's end well
- Lousy Jack and his eleven brothers
- The man who didn't believe in ghosts and
  'chantments
- The Dragon of Wantley
- Dildrum, King of the Cats
- A fairy Changeling
- A Fairy Experience
- The Goodwife of Deloraine

Other sources, especially where I might have just got one
tale from somewhere, are in the text as footnotes.

If you've enjoyed these old stories, please take a look at my book from the other side of the Pennines, "Forgotten Yorkshire Folk and Fairy Tales".

(ISBN: 978-1911500155)

Many thanks to all the Kickstarter backers who funded the production of both the "Yorkshire" and "Lancashire" versions of Forgotten Folk and Fairy Tales.

If anyone reading this book has other folk or fairy tales they know that were historically told in Lancashire or Yorkshire, I'd love to hear them and include them in future work if I can. I'm particularly interested in the "Feorin" or "Greenies" as they seem to be called in Lancashire – creatures of the "fairy realm" and people's encounters with them.

I can be found on Twitter as @Playbrarian or email at andywalsh999@gmail.com